IN DEFENSE OF THE ALIEN
Volume XII

Impacts and Consequences of IRCA; Legalization, Social Services and Health; IRCA's Employer Sanctions Provisions; Legal Immigration Reform; Refugees' Policy Issues

IN DEFENSE OF THE ALIEN
Volume XII

Impacts and Consequences of IRCA; Legalization, Social Services and Health; IRCA's Employer Sanctions Provisions; Legal Immigration Reform; Refugees' Policy Issues

Proceedings of the 1989
Annual National Legal Conference
on Immigration and Refugee Policy

Edited by Lydio F. Tomasi

1990
Center for Migration Studies
New York

CMS is an education non-profit institute founded in New York in 1964 committed to encourage and facilitate the study of the sociodemographic, economic, historical, political, legislative and pastoral aspects of human migration and refugee movements. CMS organizes an annual national legal conference on immigration and refugee policy, the proceedings of which are published in a volume series entitled IN DEFENSE OF THE ALIEN. This text represents the Twelfth Volume of that series.

IN DEFENSE OF THE ALIEN
VOLUME XII
Impacts and Consequences of IRCA; Legalization, Social Services and Health; IRCA's Employer Sanctions Provisions; Legal Immigration Reform; Refugees' Policy Issues

First Edition

Copyright © 1990 by

The Center for Migration Studies of New York, Inc.
209 Flagg Place
Staten Island, New York 10304-1199

ISBN 0-934733-43-0
ISSN 0275-634X

Library of Congress Catalog Number: 90-1536
Printed in the United States of America

CONTENTS

Introduction

U.S. Immigration policy continues to have dramatic impacts upon American society as well as upon sending countries, affecting the lives of tens of thousands of persons. The ongoing immigration reform, which U.S. Congress visits every twenty-five years or so, will usher us into the 21st Century and will greatly affect the future of our states and group relations in our country.

The effects of the Immigration Reform and Control Act of 1986 (IRCA) are beginning to have a measurable impact. Assessment and reporting on IRCA's various programs (SAWs, RAWs, SAVE, SLIAG) have already begun. And so have the complications of the second phase of legalization.

Described as "one of the great social experiments of our time," IRCA also represents a significant shift in U.S. immigration policy and law in 35 years. The underlying question of the crowded agenda of the 1989 Conference was whether the impacts of IRCA confirm the hopes of its proponents or the fears of its opponents.

While some of IRCA's provisions — such as employer sanctions — are still very much debated, some "unintended effects" of the new reform are emerging. Many undocumented aliens who did not qualify for legalization of status did not return to their native lands, and, in addition, an increasing proportion of women and children, among the latest wave of Latin American immigrants, is already beginning to strain housing, schools and health services in Texas, California, Florida and other states.

Furthermore, the issues (among others), of caps, economic requirements as a basis of immigrant visas, the point system for choosing migrants, and development policies toward sending countries are compounding the ongoing process of legal immigration reform.

Finally, U.S. refugee policy is under fire. The "immigrant character of the United States and its multi-racial makeup have kept negative attitudes" toward refugees to a lower level than in western nations, Hong Kong, Thailand and Indonesia, where acceptance rates of refugees have sunk alarmingly. In the Plan of Action submitted by UNHCR together with the U.S. and the principal resettlement countries to a 35-nation refugee conference in Kuala Lamour, Malaysia, last March, "human deterrence" policies seem to have replaced the U.N. Universal Declaration of Human Rights. With reference to the United States, recently adopted measures against Central American asylum seekers and the interdiction at sea of Haitian asylum seekers seem to undermine refugee protection.

The two-day National Legal Conference on Immigration and Refugee Policy, sponsored by the Center for Migration Studies, focused on the most salient of these current issues.

The impacts and consequences of IRCA are dealt with in Part I and II. After reviewing the legalization programs and reported fraud in the implementation of IRCA, the analysis turns to the second phase of the legalization program as well as the effects of IRCA on health care services, public education, labor market, and development in Latin America. A full examination of IRCA's employer sanctions provisions from the perspectives of government enforcing and monitoring agencies as well as of the private sector is provided in Part V.

IRCA left a number of issues unfinished. The post-1982 undocumented aliens, many in families of legal residents, continue to live within U.S. borders without political and civil rights. Newly legalized residents face long waits for legal reunion with their families given the backlogs in second preference. In addition, the issues of grounds for excluding alien visitors, are widely agreed to need revision. Furthermore, the issues of caps, economic requirements as a basis of immigrant visas, and the point system for choosing migrants are all part of the unfinished immigration agenda. Part III is devoted to the revision of U.S. legal immigration reform and issues in need of further analysis.

U.S. refugee policy has been widely criticized for its lack of even-handed treatment of refugees. Decisions about admission to the U.S. for resettlement reflect foreign policy interests almost exclusively, while humanitarian concerns seem to play secondary or tertiary roles. General issues of policy versus humanitarian interests arises concretely as the U.S. struggles with the application of the refugee definition. Soviet *perestroika*, U.S. relations with Cuba, and new political developments in Southeast Asia all raise questions about who is a refugee and how changes can be made in refugee decisions as political circumstances change. The relative need of different groups for safe haven also arises as traditional refugee sources seem to produce persons whose status is questioned and almost universally agreed to be less desperate than others who have fewer options. Part IV offers international perspectives and analyses of domestic policy issues regarding refugees.

The Conference Organizing Committee is grateful to the approximately fifty panelists from the academy, federal and state agencies, the bar, voluntary agencies and the private sector. Following a twelve-year tradition, it is our hope that the Conference remained above the emotionalism and sectarian interests inherent to immigration reform and that it continues to be an ideal forum for a rational debate in the interest of all.

Finally, I should like to acknowledge with sincere gratitude the financial assistance of the Migrant Health Program, HHS; the Center for Immigration and Population Studies of the City University of New York; the USCC Migration and Refugee Services; the National Italian American Foundation; the CWS/USA Church World Service; the Episcopal Migration Ministry; HIAS; and the Lutheran Council, USA.

Lydio F. Tomasi
Center for Migration Studies

PART I
IMPACTS AND CONSEQUENCES OF THE IMMIGRATION REFORM AND CONTROL ACT OF 1986

1

The Legalization Programs of the 1986 Immigration Reform and Control Act: Moving Beyond the First Phase[1]

SUSAN GONZALEZ BAKER AND FRANK D. BEAN
The Urban Institute

In October 1986, the U.S. Congress passed the Immigration Reform and Control Act (IRCA). One of the most significant milestones in the implementation of IRCA was reached on November 30, 1988 when the last formal application period closed for the act's legalization programs. Since IRCA's programs and provisions, which involve major changes in the way the United States deals with immigration, are scheduled for implementation over a five-year period it is too early to make definitive assessments of their final effects. However, information on the number and characteristics of immigrants applying for legalized status under IRCA provides an indication of the way the program has worked thus far and an outline of problems still to come.

THE PROGRAMS: THEIR NATURE AND SUCCESS

IRCA'S legalization programs are the largest ever implemented, with more than three million applicants. As of early spring 1989, 1.6 million applications had been approved. Additional applications are still being considered because of court challenges, and analysts expect that more than 2.7 million undocumented aliens will eventually be approved for temporary residence.

To apply for legalized status, undocumented aliens could pursue either of two routes: the general legalization program for those illegally residing in the United States since January 1, 1982 (the LAWs program), or the Special Agricultural Workers programs (the SAWs program). Applicants for the LAWs program were required to show documentation of continuous residence in the United States since January 1, 1982; upon INS approval, applicants received temporary resident status for 18 months. After that time, if the alien continues to live in the United States, meets requirements showing minimal English language and civics knowledge, and meets the health and criminal standards required of any immigrant, he or she may receive permanent alien status. Agricultural workers could apply for legalized status under two different programs, and generally they had to demonstrate they had worked at least 90 days in U.S. agriculture in the years immediately preceding passage of the legislation. The rate of approval under the LAWs program has been about 98 percent and about 94 percent under the SAWs program.

Studies of the implementation of the legalization provisions are still ongoing, but preliminary results indicate that despite some problems of publicity and outreach, the programs appear to have worked reasonably well in bringing the benefit of legal status to a quite large disadvantaged population (North and Portz, 1989; Bean, Vernez and Keely, 1989). Despite this, whether the legalization programs are judged a success is likely to be debated for some time to come and may never be settled to everyone's satisfaction. It is hard to know with certainty how many eligible undocumented aliens were in the country during the 12-month period in which applications for legalization were accepted. Pre-enrollment estimates of the number eligible ranged from 1.3 million to 2.7 million for the LAWs program and from 250,000 to 350,000 for the SAWs program. Those estimates yield a LAWs participation rate ranging from 63 percent to 100 percent, a rate that compares favorably with the experience of amnesty programs in other countries. The SAWs program enrolled applicants far beyond the numbers expected, raising widespread speculation about a high rate of fraudulent applications.

Thus, the correspondence between the numbers of expected eligible applicants and actual applications appears quite close, suggesting that the programs enrolled a substantial fraction of their targeted populations. Also, the profile of applicants matches reasonably well the profile of undocumented aliens included in the 1980 census. Overall, the distributions by age, gender, country of origin and state of residence of applicants for the legalization programs correspond with the distribution of undocumented aliens who were included in the 1980 Census, although a somewhat higher proportion of applicants came from Mexico than was the case for persons included in the census.

Several possible disincentives may have hampered participation of eligible applicants. These include: 1) fear of the Immigration and Naturalization Service (INS), 2) difficulty in meeting documentation requirements, 3) complex eligibility requirements, 4) the high cost of application ($185 per applicant), and 5) the exclusion of family members from legalization unless they were eligible on their own. The first two disincentives appear not to have been major deterrents. About seven out of ten applicants applied directly to the INS rather than through community agencies or through a lawyer, suggesting little fear of the INS. The INS showed flexibility in its documentation requirements, although on-going court challenges to some requirements may reveal that some eligible aliens may have been discouraged.

One survey of aliens identified through community and voluntary agencies that were designated by the INS to accept applications suggested that the complexity of eligibility requirements and potential applicants' lack of documentation also served to deter many from completing the application process (North and Portz, 1988). Survey respondents did not cite fear of the INS, concerns about family unity, or the expense of the process as major factors in decisions not to apply for legalization.

THE LEGALIZATION PROGRAMS AND LEGAL IMMIGRATION

Although IRCA did little to reform the legal immigration system directly, the IRCA legalization programs did provide new routes to permanent resident status for a significant number of people. Thus, IRCA introduces the potential for indirect effects on the prevailing system of visa allocation. As noted above, the approval rate for LAWs applications remains well in excess of 90 percent, translating into temporary residency status for about 1.5 million people thus far.[2] After 18 months in this temporary status, these people will be eligible to apply for permanent residence. The transition to permanent resident status brings along an entitlement to petition for immediate relatives under the second preference of the current visa allocation system. In addition, over 25,000 Haitians and 2,700 Cubans adjusted their status to permanent residence through a separate provision of IRCA and nearly 40,000 people adjusted to permanent residence through the updated registry program. All of these new permanent residents are now eligible to petition for immediate relatives. Finally, although the majority of the 1.3 million SAW applications had yet to be adjudicated at the time of this writing, at least 300,000 have been adjudicated and approved. These individuals will adjust nearly automatically to permanent residency upon completion of their temporary residency period, and will thus be entitled to petition for immediate relatives.

At first glance, it would seem that the visa allocation system faces considerable strain as this large IRCA-generated cohort of immigrants becomes eligible to initiate visa petitions. However, four factors mitigate the likelihood that large numbers of IRCA-generated petitions will occur. First, the majority of LAWs applicants have not yet made the transition from temporary to permanent resident status. This transition depends upon the temporary resident taking several additional steps, including application during a one-year eligibility period and fulfillment of an English proficiency/civics education requirement. Thus, the potential exists for some fraction of the LAWs temporary resident population to drop out of the process at each additional step along the way toward permanent residency. The result of this as yet undetermined attrition will be failure to achieve permanent residency and a return to undocumented status.

A second mitigating factor is the inhibiting effect of large backlogs under the second preference for visa allocations to Mexico, the primary source country of the IRCA beneficiaries. Similar pressures exist in such source countries as the Philippines and the Dominican Republic, both of which are represented in the top eight IRCA-immigrant source countries and are characterized as "high demand" countries for visas (Hoefer, 1989; General Accounting Office, 1989).

Third, the historically low propensity of Mexican immigrants to naturalize may also buffer the echo effect of IRCA on visa petitions. Naturalization brings an entitlement, under current immigration law, to numerically unrestricted petitions for immediate relatives, and access to a wider variety of limited visa categories. To the extent that the IRCA cohort of immigrants, largely Mexican in origin, adheres to the historical pattern of low naturalization rates, we would expect actual family-based petitions to fall short of potential petitions.

Fourth, the propensity of legal immigrants to emigrate after achieving permanent residency will affect the number of petitioners available to initiate visa requests. Pre-IRCA estimates of permanent resident emigration center at approximately 20 to 30 percent (Meissner and Papademetriou, 1988). Again, the degree to which the IRCA immigrants adhere to this pattern will affect the magnitude of the IRCA echo effect in visa petitions.

Despite these mitigating factors, some echo effect of IRCA in the visa petition profiles of the 1990s is likely to emerge, particularly for such source countries as Mexico (through legalization, SAWs and registry) and Haiti (through IRCA Cuban-Haitian adjustment). The combination of affirmative steps by Congress and the INS to create a generous legalization program, and court-mandated expansions of the legalization program to include groups initially excluded through INS regulations, has created a concentrated cohort of legal immigrants entitled to petition for relatives and employees under the prevailing system of family-based and occupationally-based visa allocation. The volume and composition of these petitions will depend on the behaviors of the petitioners, the outcome of legal immigration reform now being debated in Congress, and the cycle of conditions that serve to encourage and discourage emigration from the sending countries.

CONTINUING ISSUES IN LEGALIZATION

Phase II

Much of the media attention surrounding IRCA legalization has dissipated. Similarly, INS budgets for public information and outreach on legalization are a fraction of their Phase I levels. However, the final chapter in the story of this major innovation in U.S. immigration law has not been written. Indeed, it cannot be written while the majority of the beneficiaries have yet to complete the process. Thus, the implementation of Phase II emerges as one of the most important continuing IRCA issues.

The transition from temporary to permanent residence is not automatic for pre-1982 temporary residents. They must file their applications for permanent residency within a year of the initial eligibility date, which is eighteen months after temporary residence was granted. They must pass a test of English skills and civics knowledge or demonstrate "satisfactory pursuit" of a course of study sanctioned by the INS to attain those skills. They must demonstrate admissibility under the grounds of excludability for permanent residence — grounds which include mental illness, criminal convictions, likelihood of becoming a public charge, dangerous contagious disease (including HIV-positive test results) and history of fraudulent visa procurement or recent deportation and re-entry. If the temporary resident falls into one of these categories, a waiver must be approved for adjustment to permanent residency.

While the initial record on transition from Phase I to Phase II indicates that nearly all Phase II applicants are successfully adjusting their status, those applications represent, at present, a subset of the eligible population. As of May, 1989, only 70 percent of those who applied in May, 1987 — the first month of the LAWs program — had applied for permanent residency (Immigration and Naturalization Service, 1989a). Under current statute, their eligibility to apply for adjustment of status will end in November, 1989. Given the diversion of resources and attention to such competing INS missions as complete implementation of employer sanctions, drug interdiction, Border Patrol enforcement, refugee and asylum crises, and the constant workload of examinations and inspections, the concern has arisen that more publicity and outreach may be needed because a significant proportion of temporary residents may not be aware of or understand the second phase of the transition to permanent residency. In response, the INS has altered its regulations for the program to simplify the process, allowing applicants to file for permanent residency at any time and holding their applications until their eighteen-month temporary status has elapsed. However, no contingency plans have been announced in the event of continued low turnout as the eligibility window closes for most applicants.

Appeals

IRCA allows legalization applicants to appeal their denials for temporary or permanent resident status to an administrative appeals unit in the INS. The Legalization Appeals Unit, staffed primarily by senior immigration examiners, has examined over 13,000 cases since October, 1987. Most of these cases were remanded to the four Regional Processing Facilities for reversal based on IRCA-related litigation. However, the Legalization Appeals Unit also possesses the power to issue precedent-setting decisions on issues arising in legalization denials. With the exception of its position on denials based upon criminal histories, the Legalization Appeals Unit has adopted a generous approach to the adjudication of appeals. In recent months, the Legalization Appeals Unit has taken on such issues as the disposition of cases in which the applicant has tested positive for the Human Immunodeficiency Virus, or in which the "public interest" or "humanitarian" concerns must be defined in the granting of a waiver. On balance, their decisions have defined such issues broadly and in favor of the applicant. However, new circumstances may well arise as Phase II appeals begin (Immigration and Naturalization Service, 1989b).

Two challenges continue for the Legalization Appeals Unit: backlogs and consistency. The unit currently faces a backlog of appeals in excess of 5,000 cases. Roughly two-thirds of these cases are LAWs applications, while one-third are SAWs. With approximately 10 staffers, and the balance of SAW appeals and Phase II appeals still to come, the unit faces the backlog problem endemic to the INS in the adjudication of immigration benefits. The second challenge springs from the fact that the four INS regions are operating under different constraints from the courts in the administration of the legalization programs. For instance, the Northern, Western, and Southern regions have all altered their treatment of SAWs applications at the direction of the courts, while the Eastern region operates under a different set of conditions. When appeals from each of these regions converge upon the Legalization Appeals Unit, it becomes necessary to choose a consistent standard for adjudication. Early decisions indicate that the unit's examiners are adopting a posture more in keeping with the inclusionary tendencies to the courts.

Family Fairness

The IRCA statute itself makes no allowance for the regularization of immigration status for the family members of legalization applicants. That is, originally, an ineligible undocumented spouse or child did not enjoy any derivative benefit from the application made by an eligible family member. Less than six months into the legalization program, however, it became apparent from the slow rate of applications and the concerns voiced by the immigrant advocacy community that policymakers may have underestimated the chilling effect such a policy would have on eligible undocumented aliens who belonged to families in which some members would not qualify for legalization. As a result, the INS altered its stance, announcing a policy in October, 1987 through which ineligible children and spouses could receive "indefinite voluntary departure," allowing them to remain in the United States until their legalizing family member might be able to petition for adjustment of their status.

The policy, known as "family fairness," allows for indefinite voluntary departure for unmarried minor children if both parents have been approved for temporary residency (or one parent in the case of death or divorce).[3] Applications for ineligible spouses will be determined on a case-by-case basis if "compelling or humanitarian" factors are present. Since the policy took effect, the INS estimates that 10,644 requests have been submitted, with 5,601 requests granted (Immigration and Naturalization Service, 1989a).

One of the important subtleties of the "family fairness" policy that has not received much publicity is the fact that persons denied voluntary departure are subject to deportation. Unlike the applicants for legalization, petitioners for voluntary departure under "family fairness" enjoy no confidentiality protection. They can be placed in deportation proceedings immediately upon denial of their petitions. Indeed, instances of this occurrence are cited by the American Immigration Lawyers Association in its bulletin on "family fairness" and its consequent suggestion to members that this form of relief be pursued only on behalf of clients who have already been apprehended by INS, not on behalf of unapprehended persons. Also no standardized procedure seems to exist for the adjudication of family fairness petitions. Petitioners write letters to the District Director of the INS in their community, who may decline the petition or forward it, often to an officer in the Deportation or Investigations sections of the District Office. The lack of a standard procedure and the litmus test of "compelling or humanitarian" factors beyond the sheer hardship engendered by the break-up of the family may jointly explain the low approval rate of family fairness petitions in comparison to the other IRCA-generated forms of benefit adjudication.

DISCUSSION AND CONCLUSIONS

Of all the continuing issues in IRCA, the "family fairness" question highlights most directly one of the thorniest issues surrounding one-time-only, temporary legalization programs: What policies should be adopted toward those who do not qualify for legalization? This further raises the question: What is the size and nature of the remaining undocumented alien population in the country? Congress expected that undocumented immigrants who failed to obtain legalized status would eventually leave the United States voluntarily, because the employer sanctions provisions of the legislation, which establish civil and criminal penalties for knowingly hiring illegal aliens, would significantly reduce job opportunities for undocumented workers. As of April 1989, there is no evidence that significant numbers of undocumented aliens ineligible for legalization have departed.

Undocumented aliens who might still be in the United States fall into one of these three subgroups:

— those eligible for legalization who did not apply;

— those who arrived between January 1, 1982 — the latest date for documenting residence to be eligible for legalization — and November 6, 1986, — after which date employers had to ask for proof of legal status; and

— those who arrived after November 6, 1986 and could not obtain legal employment.

The total population of these three groups could be as little as 500,000 or as large as three million. An important task for future research is to estimate the size of this population as reliably as possible.

There is at least one reason many ineligible workers might remain in the United States. Growing disparities in job opportunities and wages between the United States and the various countries of origin make undocumented immigrants unlikely to leave voluntarily, even if job opportunities or wages worsen (Bean, Schmandt and Weintraub, 1989). Those who arrive too late to obtain legalization or to gain legal employment have several options available: self-employment, employment in firms willing to risk sanctions, possibly on substandard terms; and/or accepting longer periods of unemployment and underemployment. Many of these undocumented aliens have relatives in the United States, some of whom have been legalized, from whom they may receive support. The major burden of hardship is likely to fall more heavily on family members remaining behind in the home country, as the financial support they receive from the United States decreases. Whatever the degree of success that researchers and observers ultimately attribute to IRCA's legalization programs, a sizeable undocumented population may continue to reside in the United States.

REFERENCES

Bean, F.D., G. Vernez and C. Keely
1989   *Opening and Closing the Door: Changing U.S. Immigration Patterns and Policies.* Washington, D.C. and Santa Monica, CA: Program for Research on Immigration Policy.

Bean, F.D., J. Schmandt and S. Weintraub, eds.
1989   *Mexican and Central American Population and U.S. Immigration Policy.* Austin: CMAS Publications.

General Accounting Office
1989   "Immigration: S.358 Would Change the Distribution of Immigrant Classes." Testimony of Eleanor Chelimsky, Assistant Comptroller General, before Senate Subcommittee on Immigration and Refugee Affairs. March 3.

Hoefer, M.D.
1989   "Characteristics of Aliens Legalizing Under IRCA." Paper presented at the annual meeting of the Population Association of America. Baltimore, Maryland. March 29.

Immigration and Naturalization Service
1989a   Testimony of Alan C. Nelson, Commissioner, before House Subcommittee on Immigration, Refugees and International Law. May 17.

_____
1989b   Presentation by Francesco Isgro, Legalization Appeals Unit, at The Urban Institute Conference on Legalization. March 3.

Meissner, D.M. and D.G. Papademetriou
1988   *The Legalization Countdown: A Third-Quarter Assessment.* Washington, D.C.: The Carnegie Endowment for Peace.

North, D. and A.M. Portz
1988   *Through the Maze: An Interim Report on the Alien Legalization Program.* Washington, D.C.: Transcentury Development Associates.

_____
1989   *The U.S. Alien Legalization Program.* Washington, DC: Transcentury Development Associates.

FOOTNOTES

[1] This is a revision of a paper presented at the 12th Annual CMS National Legal Conference on Immigration and Refugee Policy, Washington, D.C., April 6-7, 1989. This paper was written under the auspices of the Program for Research on Immigration Policy, a program of public policy research and assessment in the area of immigration involving both The Urban Institute and the Rand Corporation. Core support for the Program for Research on Immigration Policy is provided by the Ford Foundation. Conclusions or opinions expressed in Program publications are those of the authors and do not necessarily reflect the views of other staff members, officers, or trustees of The Urban Institute or the Rand Corporation, advisory groups or any organizations that provide financial support to the Institute.

[2] As of this writing, approximately 193,000, I-687 applications had yet to be adjudicated.

[3] It bears noting that the term "family fairness" refers not to the families of legalization applicants, but to families outside the United States waiting for immigrant visas petitioned by their U.S. resident members. The INS took the position in announcing "family fairness" that it would not be fair to reward with a summary benefit those IRCA-ineligible family members when others had remained abroad awaiting legal entry. This position is expressed in the "case-by-case" implementation of the voluntary departure benefit to IRCA-ineligible family members.

2

Legalization Implementation: Phase II

RAYMOND B. PENN
Assistant Commissioner, Legalization
Immigration and Naturalization Service

The Immigration Reform and Control Act of 1986 (IRCA) reflected a resolve to strengthen law enforcement in order to control illegal immigration. It also reflected the nation's concerns for certain aliens who had for some time resided illegally in the United States. The theme of this legislation was focused upon regaining control of our nation's borders and eliminating the illegal alien problem in this country through the firm yet fair enforcement of our immigration laws.

The law provided for legalizing the status of millions of aliens in the United States who had been here unlawfully since before January 1, 1982, or who had been agricultural workers in the United States. The program is unique in several ways. It has provided a one time opportunity to achieve lawful permanent resident status. Applications for the benefits of the program receive confidential treatment. The general program was to be entirely funded from application fees and the adjustment to lawful status was a direct result of meeting the eligibility requirements, unlike other adjustment statutory provisions where the ultimate grant of permanent resident status was committed to agency discretion.

The Immigration and Naturalization Service (INS) took a number of steps to ensure the new legislation would be implemented effectively, efficiently and fairly. Service officials engaged in continuing dialogue with members of the public and representatives of interested organizations on how the legalization provisions of IRCA would be implemented.

The application period for the temporary resident phase of the general legalization program began on May 5, 1987, and ended on May 4, 1988. This phase of the Legalization Program was the first step for illegal aliens to become full and active members of American society and proved to be an overwhelming success with more than 1,700,000 applicants taking advantage of the opportunity to come out of the shadows.

In order to complete the process of becoming a lawful permanent resident of the United States, individuals who gained lawful temporary resident status during Phase I of the general legalization program are required to make application for such permanent resident status. The INS published an interim rule in the *Federal Register* (53 FR 43984) on October 31, 1988. Final regulations are presently prepared with publication expected by the first week in May 1989.

The final rule includes the requirements for temporary resident aliens, who are otherwise eligible, to adjust their status to that of aliens lawfully admitted for permanent residence in the United States and the procedures to be used during this process.

Under the provisions of the IRCA, a temporary resident alien may make application for permanent resident status during a twelve month period after the temporary resident has resided in the United States as such for a period of eighteen months. The service began accepting applications on November 7, 1988. Applications received anytime subsequent to the granting of lawful temporary residence, but prior to an applicant's eligibility to apply date, are being held by the service as a convenience to the public. These applications are considered "filed" on the applicant's eligibility date.

The process for the permanent resident phase of the general program will be briefly explained. For the permanent resident phase of the program, the service is utilizing a processing method that features direct mail of applications to four regional processing facilities (RPFs). After preliminary processing of applications at these facilities, applicants are interviewed at selected service offices throughout the country (including district offices, suboffices and legalization offices). The adjustment of temporary resident aliens to permanent residence consists of five major segments: pre-submission of applications; regional facility pre-interview processing; INS field and legalization office processing; post-interview regional facility processing; and immigration card facility (ICF) processing.

In the pre-submission of applications segment, INS is distributing information and forms for the adjustment to permanent resident phase of the legalization program and will continue its public information and outreach efforts for Phase II of the legalization program. The service is confident that awareness of the legalization program is high. In testimony before the Subcommittee on Immigration and Refugee Affairs, Committee on the Judiciary United States Senate, the Government Accounting Office reported that a market research study found that 92 percent of undocumented Hispanics were aware that the legalization program exists (over 84% of the legalization Phase I applicants were Hispanic). The publicity and outreach campaign for the permanent resident phase is more selective since the service knows who the temporary residents are and where they reside. In this circumstance, local level publicity and outreach methods are being employed along with national efforts.

In the Regional Processing Facility (RPF) segment, all pre-interview processing tasks are performed (*e.g.*, data entry, fee receipting, application review, scheduling of interviews, etc.). If during this review it is determined that the applicant has met all eligibility requirements (continuous residence, English language/U.S. history and government, etc.) and there was no indication of fraud in Phase I, the application may be approved. In this situation, the applicant would be notified to appear for processing at the INS Field or Legalization Office for an Alien Registration Receipt Card (I-551).

In the INS Field or Legalization Office segment, applicants are interviewed as well as processed for alien registration cards (I-551). The interview may include an English language/U.S. history and government examination for those applicants who wish to satisfy the standards for Section 312 of the Immigration and Nationality Act.

In the RPF (post-interview) segment, appeal processing and other post-interview administrative procedures occur.

Finally in the last segment of processing at the Immigration Card Facility, the I-551 is produced and the card mailed to the address specified by the alien as the place of residence. The Service began accepting Phase II applications on November 7, 1989. As of March 30, of this year, over 160,000 (10%) temporary residents have applied for permanent status.

245A PROGRAM

The application period for the general legalization program ended on May 4, 1988. The service received a total of 1,767,640 applications under this part of the program. Of these, 1,233,300 applications or about 70 percent were Mexican nationals. The second largest group was Salvadorans, with 145,600 or about 8 percent. The median age of all applicants was 30 years of age. Eighty-one percent of the total was individuals between the ages of 15 and 44, 57 percent were male and 49 percent were married.

California was the state of residence given in most of the cases (967,400 applicants, 54.7 percent), Texas was the State with the second largest claim of state of residence (314,200 applicants, 17.8 percent), New York followed with 6.8 percent, Illinois obtained 6.7 percent and Florida was the state of residence for 2.7 percent.

Under the general legalization program, those aliens granted temporary resident status must apply for permanent residence eighteen months after being granted temporary status. INS started accepting applications for permanent status on November 7, 1988. As of March 23, 1989, 155,000 temporary residents (9%) have applied for permanent status.

SAW PROGRAM

The Special Agricultural Worker (SAW) legalization program application period ended on November 30, 1988. A total of 1,300,478 applications were received during this period. Again, the highest number of applications was received from Mexican aliens, 1,054,100 or about 82 percent. The second largest group was from Haiti (49,100 or 4 percent) and El Salvador was third largest (27,800 or 2 percent). The median age of all applicants was 28 years of age. Ninety-one percent of the total was individuals between the ages of 15 and 44, and 83 percent were male and 53 percent were single.

The most predominant crops indicated were fruit and tree nuts — 38 percent with vegetables and melons making up 30 percent of all applications.

California received 691,500 (53.7%) of applications with Texas at 131,000 (10%) and Florida with 120,000 (9%).

SAWs granted temporary residence automatically convert to permanent residence status on December 1, 1989 (Group I) or December 1, 1990 (Group II). There is no application for acquiring permanent status.

RAW PROGRAM

Section 303 of IRCA provides another program for the admission of additional agricultural workers in the event it is determined there is a shortage of such workers to perform seasonal agricultural services in the United States. This is known as the Replenishment Agricultural Work Program (RAW).

During fiscal years 1990 through 1993, additional workers will be admitted to the United States if a determination is made by the secretaries of agriculture and labor that a shortage of such workers does exist in the United States. These workers will be required to perform 90 days of seasonal agricultural services for a period of three years after entry. Failure to perform such services in any of the three years will subject the alien to deportation. Permanent status will be granted if the alien meets these requirements. However, to be eligible for United States citizenship, the alien must perform 90 days of seasonal agricultural services for a period of five years.

The proposed eligibility requirements for qualifying as a RAW applicant are: 1) 18 years of age; 2) performed 20 mandays of agricultural employment in the United States between May 1, 1985 and November 30, 1988; and 3) is admissible to the United States as an immigrant.

3

Reported Fraud in the Implementation of IRCA: A Government Response

JOHN F. SHAW

Assistant Commissioner for Investigation
Immigration and Naturalization Service

Fraud is not new to the Immigration and Naturalization Service (INS). Most are aware of the 50-year tradition of the Investigations program within INS which has effectively combatted relationship fraud, occupational preference fraud, nonimmigrant visa fraud, and counterfeit, altered and fraudulently-acquired documents. Shortly after the passage of IRCA a new challenge arose: Special Agricultural Worker Program (SAW) fraud.

SAW fraud has developed mainly because of the SAW provisions of the new law which enabled an applicant to submit only an affidavit from a farmer or farm labor contractor attesting to eligibility for the benefit. This eligibility under Section 210 is based on either 90 days of work in agriculture during each of 1984, 1985 and 1986, or 90 days of work in agriculture between May 1, 1985 and May 1, 1986. Comparatively, Section 245A, the amnesty provision of the law, required extensive documentation of qualifying presence; and, consequently, ineligible aliens inclined to attempt fraud chose the relatively easier SAW application.

Although faced with reports of widespread SAW fraud during the first year after IRCA, INS was also faced with certain limiting conditions in its attempt to respond to the problem. First was the "confidentiality" provision of the law which kept INS from using information contained in these applications for any administrative enforcement purposes, although the same information could be used in a criminal prosecution. This was to encourage as many applicants as possible to apply for legalization benefits without fear of possible deportation. Since most United States attorneys are reluctant to prosecute individual fraudulent legalization applicants (because of the large numbers of those applicants and the relative lack of "jury appeal"), only the vendors of false employment affidavits and the arrangers who put the SAW applicants together with these vendors could be targeted.

Secondly, the additional personnel that had been allocated were earmarked to be used only in the implementation of employer sanctions. Consequently, no additional officers were provided to undertake these additional and, as we have learned, pervasive cases of fraud. Without augmentation of personnel, ways were sought to more efficiently and effectively detect and limit the fraud through enhanced coordination with the intelligence and legalization programs.

Despite these limitations, investigations have been very successful in the interdiction of fraud in the legalization program. One of the most productive collaborative efforts has been the collection and analysis of data from all SAW applications by intelligence personnel posted at each of the four Regional Processing Facilities, where SAW applications are adjudicated. The correlation of information on these applications has resulted in the discovery of many schemes which would otherwise not have been detected, many of them crossing district and regional boundaries. The resulting leads pertaining to these schemes are provided directly to investigations personnel at the appropriate district offices. These leads, and others which come from informants or employees of the local legalization office, have formed the basis of the INS's considerable success in the interdiction of fraud in the legalization program. Specifically, with the officer-hour equivalent of 132 agents dedicated to fraud of all kinds, personnel have investigated more than 700 SAW fraud cases resulting in 136 convictions of SAW document vendors and arrangers since the passage of IRCA and without slighting other areas of fraud.

So, who are these SAW fraud vendors and arrangers? They range from persons of simple means, to prominent well-respected members of communities, to individuals with previous convictions for drugs or weapons trafficking. "Operation Brown Widow," a Charlotte, N.C. investigation, targeted a United States citizen woman who was alleged to sell false affidavits of empl yment on her farm for 250 dollars each. Through an informant, several Hispanic INS special agents were introduced to the document vendor. After the agents waited in line for two hours with other customers, they made and recorded three document purchases. These purchases were used to justify a search warrant which was executed at the time of the vendor's arrest. The search yielded two filing cabinets containing approximately 800 false SAW employment records. While awaiting trial on these charges, the defendant was released on bail, and thereafter absconded. She subsequently surrendered several months later and, on August 19, 1988, was convicted of one violation of fraud in application for SAW benefits (Title 8, USC 1160).

Another case, at the other end of the spectrum, is "Operation Takedown," a joint Los Angeles/Fresno investigation. The arrest of two SAW document vendors, working together in Los Angeles, resulted in sufficient information to obtain a search warrant for the farm of the individual in the Fresno area who provided the false employment affidavits. The search of the farm resulted in the discovery of a "crack" and methamphetamine lab, the seizure of 150 pounds of narcotics and the arrest of five other individuals involved in the sale of the false SAW documents, two of whom were also operating the illegal lab and distributing the narcotics. To date, five convictions have been obtained.

An example of the extent of a single SAW fraud scheme is "Operation Mongoose." This case involves a large loosely constructed conspiracy of arrangers and document suppliers who sell false SAW employment affidavits primarily to Indians and Pakistanis for fees between 3,000 and 4,000 dollars per document packet. The New York office has worked closely with officers in Miami, San Antonio, Washington, D.C. and Newark, resulting in 11 arrests in New York, 7 arrests in Texas, 2 arrests in Virginia, 1 arrest in New Jersey, and 7 arrests in Miami; with leads developed on 10 additional targets in New York who have ties to other vendors in Florida and California. As of March 1989, five convictions in this case have been obtained and more are expected. Businesses get involved in SAW fraud too. In "Operation Green Thumb," the Washington office brought multiple counts of SAW fraud, visa fraud, and conspiracy and harboring of illegal aliens against a lawn care firm in Fairfax, Virginia. The company, which had provided false SAW documents as part of the harboring activity, was sentenced to pay a 30,000 dollar fine for violations of employer sanctions law and 7,250 dollars in restitution to the SAW applicant employees.

In addition, a supervisory employee was sentenced to one year probation and a 2,000 dollar fine. An administrative fine of over 50,000 dollars remains pending.

These accomplishments are dwarfed by the extent of probable fraud. A recent report shows that over 200,000 pending SAW applications are suspect by virtue of a connection to known or suspected vendors or arrangers. Investigations undertaken to date encompass only about one-fifth of those cases. Progress in reducing the number of pending suspect cases is hindered by two facts: first, pursuant to regulations and ensuing administrative appeal review, INS may not deny suspect cases for fraud unless fraud is proven in each case; and secondly, that investigations must, out of necessity, concentrate its resources on the vendors and arrangers of fraudulent documentation instead of individual applicants.

Nonetheless, investigation of SAW vendors and arrangers will be continued. They are still out there selling SAW documents for applicants to submit as supplemental documentation for the applications they filed before the November 30, 1988 deadline. Placing emphasis on SAW document vendors, throughout the five-year statute of limitations if necessary, will not only yield prosecutions of vendors involved in SAW fraud and additional denials of relating, pending, SAW cases for fraud, but will have a greater impact as well.

Many of the SAW document vendors did not just take up this line of work with the passage of IRCA. They had been in the document-vending business years before, providing false or counterfeit green cards, other immigration documents, birth certificates and even United States passports to illegal aliens. We also know that some who did begin their new profession with the SAW program have since moved on to the sale of other documents which can be used to circumvent employer sanctions law, or to enable many other illegal activities.

There is good news and bad news here: the SAW period in immigration history has enabled many vendors to learn their trade and hone their skills; the good news is that, because SAW cases involve the full range of complexity and such a variety of circumstances, this period in immigration history has also enabled investigative agents, both the experienced and the newly hired, to perfect their skills, both traditional and technical, as never before. The result is that fraudulent document vendors who attempt to grow rich through such deceitful and exploitative activity will be sought out wherever possible and prosecuted to the maximum extent.

PART II
LEGALIZATION, SOCIAL SERVICES AND HEALTH

4

Bringing Immigrants into the Health Care System

JOHN W. MCFARLAND
Migrant Health Program

The task of bringing immigrants into the mainstream of health care delivery offered in the United States today provides an enormous challenge. Today's immigrants are multiethnic and have a variety of needs and points of access. There are a few constructive models which would maximize present resources, and provide a foundation with which to address continuity of care issues.

The Migrant Health Program, funded through the Public Health Service Section 329, provides an interesting and functional example of a system which should be examined for its relevance as a model to facilitate delivery of health care to immigrants.

What are the similarities between the migrant farmworker population and other world migration populations? One of the similarities is that agricultural labor continues to be the source of employment which remains on the bottom rung of the socioeconomic ladder. Therefore, new populations coming into the United States, for example, as well as many other countries around the world, often make their occupational debut in farm labor. This is most classically demonstrated by the continuing flow of immigrants from Mexico and Central America to the United States, the arrival of Asians on the West Coast who have been incorporated temporarily into the California agricultural workforce and the migration of farmworkers from the Caribbean basin area into the East Coast migrant stream.

Other similarities between migrant farmworkers and immigrants are the barriers to access and utilization of health services which include:

— lack of available patient dollars with which to purchase services;

— disenfranchisement;
— cultural differences from the local community;
— socioeconomic status;
— language differences as a barrier to effective communication;
— lack of experience in dealing with modern health delivery systems;
— legal status;
— lack of adequate public resources to meet the need; and
— mobility and housing barriers.

Migrant farmworkers are just one subset of this country's migrating population. If we look at this subset we can see that it is a population for which public awareness has had greater heights. At this time, more than a decade after the plight of *compasinos* and farm laborers was brought to the attention of the American public many of the problems remain basically what they were twenty/thirty years ago.

There is a movement within a small group of health providers in this country who have used the example of networking as the impetus for the creation of a grass-roots movement to work on behalf of migrant farm laborers across the country. This grass-roots movement has resulted in the establishment of an organization called the Migrant Clinicians Network which is comprised of health providers from 400 health centers around the country that prioritize delivery of health care services to migrant and seasonal farmworkers. These providers comprise a multidisciplinary team of doctors, dentists, nurses, health educators, social workers, pharmacists, nutritionists and lay health providers. This organization, established in 1984, currently has a small staff and operates under the umbrella of a larger organization, the National Migrant Referral Project. After two years of functioning on a voluntary basis, the organization received 5,000 dollars of funding. In the following years, this organization has assumed a more formalized structure with broad base support and has been very successful in developing a set of services and products which are available to migrant health centers around the country. Workable solutions to the problems which migrant farmworkers and immigrants encounter have been developed and include:

— enhanced understanding, public relations and public awareness;
— advocacy at all levels;
— matching expectations of health providers to realities of this population, *i.e.*, orientation;
— networking and the development of collaborative working relationships and the creation of affiliations with mainstream service delivery systems;

— use of successful Third World models to create positive change; and
— culturally and linguistically appropriate preventive health education specifically targeted to high risk subsets of the immigrant
population.

The primary purpose of the Migrant Clinicians Network is to identify and
address issues which impact on the health status of migrant and seasonal
farmworkers. Our goal is to access and modify, where necessary, the current
health care delivery system to better meet the needs of this population. This
network serves as the national clinical forum for migrant and seasonal
farmworker health issues, and also as a resource for clinicians, health centers,
allied public and private agencies, and the Migrant Health Program at the
local, regional and central office level.

Examining the specific endeavor developed in order to address national
continuity in the area of disease and health prevention is the adoption of a
set of health objectives for the beginning of the 21st century which are
specific to the migrant and seasonal farmworker population. Through this
endeavor, which required a coordinated effort of education, public awareness, testimony and development of health policy, we will create a
foundation for consensus and focus for the next ten years.

One of the priorities for the Migrant Clinicians Network over the coming
thirty-six months is the identification of important arenas for research within
the migrant and seasonal farmworker population, and the identification of
dollar resources and interested qualified researchers to aid us in this effort.
This research agenda will allow us to move forward with creating a foundation for greater public awareness and interface to allow us to work
collaboratively together to meet these needs.

The Migrant Clinicians Network welcomes this opportunity to work with
a group of persons interested in the global issues of national and international immigration. Hopefully, the Network's efforts and successes
regarding migrant and seasonal farmworkers can be helpful in designing
models for application to other migrating populations.

5

The Effects of IRCA/SLIAG on Public Education: The California Experience

LINDA J. WONG

California Tomorrow

At the start of the legalization program in May 1987, state policymakers realized that the Immigration Reform and Control Act of 1986 (IRCA) would have a significant impact on California, since an estimated one-half of the nation's undocumented immigrants were thought to be living in the state. The legislature therefore directed the California Postsecondary Education Commission (CPEC) in its 1988/89 Budget Act to conduct a study on "eligible legalized aliens" (ELAs) needing English and civics instruction to meet the requirements for permanent resident status.[1] The goals of the report were to obtain more data on the ELA population, analyze the availability and adequacy of amnesty educational programs and offer recommendations for future education funding.

In October 1988, CPEC contracted with California Tomorrow, a nonprofit organization, to do the survey work. Work began immediately thereafter. Telephone interviews were conducted with 89 percent of the education service providers funded under the State Legalization Impact Assistance Grants (SLIAG), half of the providers with pending SLIAG applications and 44 percent of the nonapplicant providers. At the same time, indepth interviews were conducted in ten communities throughout the state, reflecting both urban and rural areas, to examine the implementation process and the problems encountered in matching need with services. In addition, relevant state files, documents and plans were reviewed, along with available state and federal data on the implementation of IRCA. Finally, key state officials, immigration experts and educators were interviewed to identify the major issues in designing, implementing and coordinating state educational programs.

A preliminary draft of the report was prepared in December 1988. A second draft was submitted in March 1989. The final report, published in May 1989, had statistics current as of January 27, 1989 from the Immigration and Naturalization Service (INS), which were previously unavailable.[2]

In general, the study found that statewide capacity was adequate to meet the demand for English and civics instruction. However, there was a serious shortfall in some communities, with a significant mismatch between need and available services. These problems arose in part because state planning processes began well before the start of the legalization program, when there were no federal regulations and little information about the educational backgrounds of legalization applicants. As a result, state officials underestimated the size of the amnesty population and the number of people needing language instruction. This in turn created a funding shortfall which delayed the expansion of existing programs and the creation of new ones. They also did not anticipate the huge demand in the early stages of phase two, which aggravated the capacity problem in some heavily impacted communities.[3] Despite these obstacles, however, the California program was more comprehensive than most and moved more quickly than others in the country.

NEED AND AVAILABILITY ISSUES

"Need" is a difficult term to define. It is at once a subjective evaluation of what a person thinks (s)he requires and an assessment of what (s)he hopes to accomplish. Thus, in the context of the legalization program, some ELAs needed educational services to qualify for permanent resident status, while others wanted coursework to develop their English language skills to become more employable. The state education plan articulated both of these objectives: to meet the immediate need of helping ELAs qualify for the second phase of legalization, and to open the doors to longer term educational opportunity. Initial planning decisions were based on rough estimates of the number of people applying for legal status, the number receiving approval, and assumptions about their educational backgrounds and needs and INS standards for proficiency in meeting the criteria for permanent status.

Number of Legalization Applicants

In developing estimates on the number of ELAs in need of educational services, data from the INS Legalization Application Processing System (LAPS) were utilized. As of January 27, 1989, INS had 1,416,148 applications in the LAPS database. Pending applications not yet in the system brought the total to approximately 1.66 million, of whom 967,000 were pre-1982 immigrants and 691,500 were seasonal agricultural workers (SAWs). After reducing the figures to reflect INS approval rates for the two legalization programs and narrowing the age range of applicants to between 16 and 64 (the group required by INS to demonstrate a basic proficiency in English and civics), the total ELA population came to 1,476,370, of whom 856,271, or 58 percent, were pre-1982 applicants and 620,099, or 42 percent, were SAWs (*See* Table 1).

TABLE 1

ESTIMATED NUMBER OF ELIGIBLE LEGALIZED ALIENS IN CALIFORNIA AGED 16-64

Total: 1,476,370

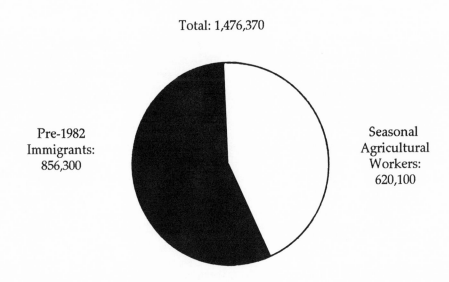

Pre-1982
Immigrants:
856,300

Seasonal
Agricultural
Workers:
620,100

Note: Adjudicated approval and denial rates utilized in this formula are actual rates to date (97.2 percent for pre-1982 immigrants and 93.9 percent for seasonal agricultural workers). These rates reflect 75 percent of "pre-1982" applications adjudicated and only 27 percent of seasonal agricultural worker applications. There is reason to expect that denial rates will rise, particularly among seasonal agricultural worker applicants, over the next six-month period. Unofficial estimates of these expected denial rates are as high as 50 percent. Richard Epstein of the department of Health and Welfare suggests a 25 percent denial rate as a working figure for projections. Applying this high denial rate would lower the number of seasonal agricultural workers by 94,000 to 526,000.

Source: California Tomorrow.

Nearly 60 percent of the state's ELA population between the ages of 16 and 64 were found in just three counties: Los Angeles, Orange and San Diego (*See* Table 2). There were, however, seventeen other counties with ELA populations of more than 10,000.

TABLE 2

PROJECTED ELAS AGED 16-64 IN THE LARGEST COUNTIES,
ADJUSTED TO INCLUDE UNPROCESSED APPLICATIONS AND
APPROVAL RATES AFTER ADJUDICATION

County	Pre-1982	SAWs	Total
Los Angeles	562,298	112,985	675,283
Orange	79,726	31,733	111,459
San Diego	34,541	62,103	96,644
Subtotal	676,565	206,821	883,386
State Total	856,300*	620,100*	1,476,370

* Rounded to nearest hundred.

Source: Legalization Application Processing System and Statistical Analysis Branch, Immigration and Naturalization Service

Two-thirds of all ELAs were male (combining both pre-1982 and SAWs), and the overwhelming majority were Hispanic: 82 percent came from Mexico, 8 percent from El Salvador, 2 percent from other Central American countries and the remaining 8 percent represented other nationalities. Fewer than 1 percent of the ELAs came from English speaking nations.

Educational Backgrounds of ELAs

State agencies responsible for the IRCA planning process operated in a virtual data vacuum. There were no accurate figures on the number of second phase amnesty filings; there was no demographic profile of the legalization population, since little was known about undocumented immigrants; and INS did not issue its "interim final" regulations on permanent residence until November 1988 — much too late for state planning purposes. State officials therefore had to base their planning data on estimates derived from non-IRCA students already enrolled in adult English-as-a-Second Language (ESL) programs, the state's Hispanic population and existing background information on Mexican permanent residents. In the meantime, national estimates prepared by the Refugee Policy Group and the National Council of La Raza indicated that as many as 77 percent of the total ELA population had little or no proficiency in English and significant numbers were not literate in their native tongue. These estimates, combined with reports from local education service providers in the state, confirmed the opinions of many that the need for educational programs would be great.

Scenarios of Need

Given the state's short-and long-term interests in providing access to educational services, it was apparent that a single "need" figure was not enough. So three separate scenarios of need were developed (*See* Table 3). The first scenario consisted of a minimum estimate based on the number of pre-1982 immigrants between the ages of 16 and 64 in need of classes to satisfy the second phase requirements; this figure came to 856,271. Securing a more precise number beyond the total pre-1982 population was difficult, because of ambiguous and changing INS regulations, and the level of knowledge needed to meet the phase two requirements and delays in developing test options to regular enrollment in a course of study were unclear.

The confusion was further compounded when a policy conflict emerged between educators who wanted immigrants to develop actual proficiency in English and immigration officials and immigrant rights advocates who did not want the language requirements to become a stumbling block to permanent resident status. Despite these differences of opinion, however, the reality was that many ELAs believed they needed coursework, because they wanted to be safe. Even though some had a basic grasp of the language and had other means of learning American government and history, they felt that taking a class offered the best assurance of satisfying the INS requirements, and safety was a form of need.

The second scenario consisted of a likely demand for educational services based on available data on the educational histories and current enrollment patterns of ELAs. This group of applicants enrolled in classes not only to satisfy the permanent residence requirements, but to achieve other educational goals as well, whether it was to learn more English, apply for eventual citizenship or to enhance their employment skills. As a result of these additional reasons, they enrolled in larger numbers than expected and stayed longer in the classroom. This scenario also took into account the entire pre-1982 population and an additional 25 percent of the farmworkers who might enroll (even though they were not required to meet the same language and civics requirements), thus resulting in a figure of just over 1 million people.

Finally, a third possible scenario had to be considered. Since little was known about the ELAs' use of educational services and because the situation was so fluid, the state had to consider the possibility that all ELAs, pre-1982s

and farmworkers would want access to educational programs. This last
scenario therefore included the entire universe of ELAs aged 16 to 64 in
California, or 1.5 million people.

TABLE 3

THREE SCENARIOS OF CALIFORNIA'S NEED FOR
EDUCATIONAL SERVICES FOR ELIGIBLE LEGALIZED ALIENS,
USING JANUARY 27,1989, DATA FROM THE
IMMIGRATION AND NATURALIZATION SERVICE

	Scenario 1	Scenario 2	Scenario 3
Pre-1982 immigrants aged 16-64 who need educational services in order to adjust to permanent residency status	856,271		
Expected demand for educational services		1,011,304	
Potential demand for educational services by all legalized aliens eligible under the Immigration Reform and Control Act			1,476,370

Notes: The Scenario 2 and 3 numbers may be lower if the application denial rate of seasonal
agricultural workers increases. At an estimated 25 percent denial rate, Scenario 2 would total
988,000 and Scenario 3 would total 1,382,000.

Source: California Tomorrow.

Capacity

Implementation of IRCA's legalization provisions and its English language
requirements for permanent residency came at a time when there was already
an explosive demand for ESL services. With a foreign-born population of 5.3
million residents, the state's educational institutions were heavily impacted
by newcomers. In 1986/87, for example, ESL courses represented about 40
percent of the adult education average daily attendance (ADA) and about 38
percent of community college non-credit ADA. Consequently, IRCA's phase
two educational requirements placed further strain on an already burdened
service delivery system. Despite the intensity of demand and the pressure to
move quickly, however, only 32 percent of the surveyed providers had no
operational programs prior to their involvement in IRCA.

The projected supply of amnesty classes was in constant flux, reflecting an interplay of factors which change over time, including varying levels of student demand, the availability of qualified teachers, the availability of physical space, administrative capacity, adequacy of funding and reimbursement mechanisms, and institutional commitment to the program. Based on information from adult education programs, community colleges and community organizations on the number of ELAs they could serve, the SLIAG-funded provider system had a capacity to help approximately 1,082,000 people. Outside the SLIAG system, education providers had an additional 18,000 seats available. Thus, total capacity was estimated to be 1.1 million slots over a three-year period, from 1987-1990. Comparing availability with demand, the statewide supply seemed adequate under scenarios #1 and #2. However, when these slots were located and matched up with demand, there was a serious mismatch at the county level.

Under scenario #1, 37 counties out of a total of 58 had a shortfall of seats. Seven counties were considered critical in that the shortage was in excess of 1,000 slots.[4] Under scenario #2, 24 counties with a total of 15,000 ELAs had no SLIAG providers at all, and another 24 counties reported a shortage of classes. Of the latter, 20 counties were considered critical, in which the shortage was in excess of 1,000 slots. Only 10 counties statewide had the capacity to meet the full demand for ESL and civics instruction.[5]

By far the largest providers were the adult education programs run by local school districts. They alone served 76 percent of the ELAs in fiscal year 1988/89. Community organizations in the meanwhile assisted an additional 13 percent of the immigrants, and community colleges served the remaining 11 percent. Without exception, providers in each of these categories had waiting lists: 53 percent of adult education programs; 50 percent of the community colleges; and 68 percent of the community organizations. Finding out who was enrolled in these classes turned out to be more difficult than expected. It was not possible to separate the pre-1982 cohort from SAWs, or ELAs from non-ELAs, because many providers did not give priority to the pre-1982 cohort, and they did not draw distinctions between the two groups of legalization applicants.

Length of Enrollment

When INS drafted the regulations on phase two, no one could predict whether ELAs would stay in the classroom just long enough to get the certificate of satisfactory pursuit or remain for the full term of an educational program. Survey responses from ESL providers indicated that both possibilities were likely. They said that many immigrants were in fact staying beyond the 40 hours of instruction, which provided strong evidence that they wanted to learn English and achieve other educational objectives. If they dropped out for some reason, they re-enrolled at rates much higher than expected. For example, community colleges reported 155 hours as the average length of stay; community organizations reported 116 hours; and adult education programs (excluding the Los Angeles Unified School District, which is the single largest provider in the state) averaged 97 hours of instruction. Overall, enrollment averaged about 130 hours.

These longer-than-expected attendance levels showed that ELAs were using the classes not just to satisfy the INS requirements, but to pursue broader educational objectives as well. While this was good news for educators, it also meant a slower turnover rate, since ELAs were staying in the classroom for longer periods of time. Additionally, ELAs were filling slots more than once, since they could return for a second year of instruction. Consequently, the number of available slots did not — and could not — relate directly to the number of ELAs served.

Timing of Demand

In the early planning stages for SLIAG, neither state officials nor service providers were certain about the phasing of demand for classes. The Department of Finance used and 80-hour per ELA attendance average as the basis for its 1988/89 SLIAG education budget and further assumed this attendance level would remain constant over the life of SLIAG. Many providers, on the other hand, made conflicting assumptions about the timing issue. For example, 41 percent of the providers responding to the California Tomorrow survey anticipated an eventual decline in enrollment, while 35 percent expected an increase. The large providers foresaw 1988/89 as the peak year, with utilization declining in 1989/90. Some believed there would be an initial panic, with the situation calming down considerably once INS had its certification and testing procedures in place and public awareness of the requirements increased. Others thought that enrollment patterns would parallel the timetable for the second phase of legalization. Still others (including providers in counties with significant shortages of programs) expected a decline in enrollment. In all cases, however, these assumptions were made in an information vacuum.

If utilization of educational services is related to the need to satisfy the immigration service's phase two requirements, then demand for ESL and civics instruction should peak in late 1990 and end by January 1991, when the second phase of legalization comes to a close. However, to the extent that ELAs use educational services beyond the required minimum, demand is more likely to grow than diminish with the passage of time. This is especially true if ELAs decide to pursue a high school diploma, go on to higher education or enroll in vocational education courses.

Barriers to Creating New Programs or Expanding Current Ones

Expansion of current programs was hampered by several factors, including inadequate funding levels, limited administrative capacity, shortage of classroom space and lack of qualified teachers. Of all these reasons, however, inadequate reimbursement rates and complicated funding procedures were the most often heard complaints.

The state Department of Education had set the reimbursement rate at $2.59 per instructional hour, which was the rate normally allocated to adult education programs based on average daily attendance (ADA). This rate was lower than what community colleges usually receive under their state ADA formula, which is $2.85 an hour, and did not take into account start-up costs or other expenses which new and existing programs had to incur. Consequently, low funding rates, coupled with delays in the reimbursement process, discouraged many providers from expanding their current programs.

For providers outside the SLIAG system, a preference for dealing with known and predictable funding sources (either the state ADA or other operating funds) was the main reason for not becoming a part of the federal program. Many expressed a desire to stay with the state ADA because it was already in place, funds were certain, and risks were minimal; in the case of community colleges, another reason was the higher state reimbursement rate.

Education programs which did not serve legalization applicants mentioned three reasons for not expanding their services: 1) an unwillingness to deal with federal funding and its requirements; 2) lack of evidence of a high demand for classes; and 3) no priority to serve this population of students. However, one-half of the surveyed providers who were not involved in SLIAG wanted more information about the need for classes and the availability of funding. Apparently, some did not know about SLIAG, while others thought the supply of classes was adequate, even though they were in counties with a significant shortage of programs. Based on these responses, it was clear that more outreach had to be done in order to bring a larger number of providers into the system.

ISSUES OF QUALITY

Because the 40-hour requirement for a certificate of satisfactory pursuit implied that attendance was more important than acquisition of actual proficiency, educators expressed a concern about the quality of services offered. Many programs were designed as off-campus, short-term efforts operating at significantly lower costs than regular educational programs. Consequently, there were widespread fears that "certificate mills" would spring up and not provide students with genuine learning opportunities. To access the quality of educational services the study examined several factors, including class size, teacher qualifications, adequacy of curriculum and materials, and level of support services, to name a few.

Class Size

The education plan developed by the state Department of Education called for an optimal class size of no more than 25 students. But an unexpected demand, coupled with slow start-up and funding delays, made large and overcrowded classrooms inevitable. At the time of the survey, the statewide average was 35, with some classes as large as 75 to 100 students. Because the need was greatest at the beginning levels of ESL, enrollment was heaviest in these courses, which therefore experienced the worst overcrowding.

Teachers

Overall, providers did not encounter any major problems in finding qualified teachers. During the initial stages of phase two, an estimated 92 percent of the hired teachers had credentials and 86 percent had previous experience. Of the three major categories of providers, adult education programs had the least difficulty finding instructors, since they could draw from the ranks of elementary and secondary school professionals. On the other hand, community organizations had the hardest time recruiting qualified personnel, because of their inability to compete with salaries and benefit packages offered by local school districts, and their lack of access to an infrastructure from which to attract a supply of teachers. In addition, community colleges had a more difficult time than public schools, because they were limited to part-time instructors. In their case, the need to gear up quickly and a desire to minimize costs necessitated a hiring process which avoided lengthy tenure review, committee clearances and affirmative action requirements — all of which were involved if full-time personnel were sought.

While the teachers were generally qualified, they were often unprepared to meet the specific needs of ELAs. Few were familiar with the legalization program and the requirements for permanent residency. Some had extensive background teaching ESL but none in American government or history. Others had a hard time coping with large numbers of preliterate and illiterate students. To fill these gaps, programs spent a lot of time and resources on staff development. Over 93 percent of the providers offered some kind of in-service training on the legalization process and INS requirements. They also developed teaching methodologies for beginning levels of ESL, assisted instructors in finding ways to incorporate civics into the ESL curriculum and provided insight into the cultural backgrounds of legalization applicants. Because as many as half of the enrollees were preliterate in English, technical assistance in developing new approaches, curriculum and materials was identified as the greatest area of need.

Curriculum

Not surprisingly, nearly all the programs reported a shortage of materials for use with preliterate adults. More specifically, teachers lacked usable materials on civics and government and those reflecting the immigrant experience and the bridging of cultures and nations. Some programs had good resource centers and developed information networks to share their new curricula with others. But the networks were limited in scope or were restricted to people in state-affiliated or professional associations. Consequently, some providers, mainly those affiliated with community organizations, were left out.

Support Services

All providers stressed the importance of support services to facilitate the use of educational programs. They range from childcare to transportation, counseling and orientation. Nearly nine out of ten SLIAG providers said they offered support services of some kind, in addition to academic instruction. Most of the services consisted of educational and phase two counseling. Of all the services provided, the most important — and the most lacking — was daycare. Only 36 percent of the programs had any kind of childcare services. This meant that many students had to bring their children to class; but more likely than not, it meant they attended class only sporadically or not at all. Since women were already underrepresented in the ELA population, their ability to navigate the waters of phase two could be jeopardized by the absence of daycare, which would otherwise facilitate their enrollment in class.

State Support Mechanisms

In October 1987, the state Department of Education estimated that 11 staff positions would be needed to implement the SLIAG-funded programs for 1987/88. A year later, only four of these positions had been filled. The resulting staff shortage in the state IRCA unit caused serious problems, ranging from significant delays in the development of policies and procedures to a slow-down in the processing and approval of SLIAG applications. The latter had an especially adverse effect on providers, because the long turn-around time aggravated the cash-flow problems of many agencies. In short, the quality of the state program was compromised, because the technical assistance so desperately needed at the local level was not forthcoming from government officials.

Key State Issues

In reviewing California's implementation of SLIAG, two issues affected the state's ability to perform. The first was IRCA's silence on the state role in implementing immigration reform, and the second dealt with the designation of a single agency to distribute funds to others. IRCA's legislative history seemed to envision a limited role for states, relegating them to a fiscal "watchdog" and "pass through" function for federal funds. While it was understandable that Congress wanted flexibility in allowing states to define their own roles in implementing IRCA, the absence of congressional intent language in the statute meant that states had no clear guidance on their responsibility for planning program delivery or in managing the long-term effects of IRCA on a state's educational system and its economy. While elements of these broader policy issues were present in the state planning process, officials by and large confined themselves to the short-term goals of dispensing funds to local governments and getting programs off the ground.

On the issue of a single state agency managing SLIAG, this approach, while more efficient from a federal perspective, created some serious jurisdictional conflicts because of California's governance structure. Under the state constitution, both the Governor and the State Superintendent of Instruction are separately elected constitutional officers. The Governor oversees the operations of executive branch agencies, which include Health and Welfare, and the Superintendent heads the Department of Education. By designating the Health and Welfare Agency as the primary administrator of SLIAG and by requiring the state Department of Education to be responsible for the delivery of educational services, the federal government forced the state to cut across agency lines when making decisions, thus setting the stage for jurisdictional conflicts. These conflicts emerged in the summer of 1987, and continued through the fall of 1988. They centered mainly on the issue of funding: how much money should be allocated to education and when these funds would be disbursed.

When the Congressional Budget Office prepared its cost estimates for the House version of immigration reform, it concluded that education would be the single largest component of costs arising under the legalization program — an estimated 3 billion dollars out of a total 5 billion dollars.[6] IRCA eventually set aside 10 percent of the federal funds for education but allowed the states to exceed this amount.[7] The staff of the state Health and Welfare Agency first proposed to allocate the statutory minimum of 175 million dollars of the estimated 1.75 billion dollars it would receive for educational purposes. In contrast, the state Department of Education wanted between 459.2 and 530.2 million dollars for adult education services, with the lower figure excluding farmworkers from its educational programs, and the higher figure including them. The haggling eventually came to an end when the Governor and the Superintendent of Education reached a compromise of 351 million dollars, which could be used like a line of credit and drawn upon as needed. When the state legislature ratified this amount and incorporated it into the 1988/89 Budget Act, it also limited the administration's ability to reallocate funds among the health, education and public assistance categories. Consequently, the Budget Act language appeared to nullify the agreement between the Governor and Superintendent by limiting 1988/89 education expenditures to no more than 84.5 million dollars.

FUNDING ISSUES

Important funding issues facing the state were threefold: first, whether overall funding for education was adequate; second, whether the timing of funds was sufficient to meet the demand; and third, whether the state's funding formulas and reimbursement procedures were adequate and appropriate.

The total education budget of 351 million dollars was based on a series of assumptions about the demography of legalization applicants and INS requirements for permanent residency, as well as educated guesses about immigrants' use of educational services. Because accurate INS figures on the ELA population were not available until the end of 1988, the Population Research Unit of the state Department of Finance had to continually revise its ELA estimates, starting with 655,000 in July 1987, to 1.3 million in July of 1988 to a total of 1.7 million in January 1989. For SLIAG purposes, the state underestimated the number of pre-1982 applicants by nearly 20 percent and SAWs by a huge 300 percent. At the same time, it undercounted ELAs in the 16-64 age range; instead of the anticipated 79 percent, the actual percentage turned out to be much higher, at 91 percent.

Further, the Department of Finance estimated that 80 percent of the ELAs would enroll in classes and that 10 percent would drop out; of those enrolled, it assumed that attendance would average 80 hours. At the time of the study, there was no information to confirm the former assumption, but the latter estimate of 80 hours of attendance was clearly too low, based on field reports that ELAs were in class for an average of 130 hours. Moreover, state planners did not anticipate the initial surge of demand for educational services and assumed instead that usage would remain constant over a five-year period. Consequently, the projected number of ELAs enrolling in class in 1988/89 turned out to be four times higher than the budget estimate for that fiscal year.

Aside from these major estimation discrepancies, funding formulas and reimbursement rates were other problems which plagued the SLIAG program. Federal funding for amnesty education was based on a reimbursement schedule. This meant that providers had to have sufficient cash reserves to absorb the initial costs until their claims could be paid by the state. Since the reimbursement rate of $2.59 per instructional hour was tied to the adult school ADA, it placed community colleges and community organizations at a distinct disadvantage. The colleges had no incentive to use the federal funds if they could support the ESL programs out of their regular state ADA of $2.85 per instructional hour. For those already above their state spending limit, the low SLIAG reimbursement rate became a major obstacle which deterred many colleges from getting involved.

Community organizations, on the other hand, faced a different set of financial problems. Unlike the large providers, they had to create whole new infrastructures by making substantial capital investments in securing space, equipment and materials. They also incurred sizeable start-up costs in order to find instructors and develop the administrative capacity to handle the programs. At the same time, they had to contend with fewer sources of support and smaller cash reserves. Consequently, prolonged delays in reimbursing their claims usually resulted in serious cash flow problems, which in turn led to program cutbacks. To eliminate these barriers and encourage more providers to enter the SLIAG system, the state not only had to address the problem of the funding formula, but increase the allotment for assessment and start-up costs, speed up the reimbursement process and broaden the definition of reimbursable expenses.

CONCLUSION

Upon completion of the study, several recommendations were made to the state legislature. Among them, the state was urged to: address the funding shortfall for education; establish priority enrollment for pre-1982 applicants in counties with a shortage of classes; provide legislative oversight and long-term planning; improve the quality of state-level planning and coordination among state agencies; institute high-level involvement by the state Department of Education; and adjust the funding formulas to adequately reflect actual costs and program needs.

While these recommendations were directed to the state, they have implications for Congress as well. The main one is IRCA's long-term effects on education. For the first time, high school students who are also legalization beneficiaries have an opportunity to go to college. Lawful residency not only provides them with long-term security and a permanent future in this country, it also makes them eligible for federally-funded financial aid.[8] At the same time, adults who have enrolled in ESL classes are more likely to return to school for other educational services, whether in the area of language instruction, general education, vocational education, job training or higher education. The SLIAG funds are not permanent and were never intended as such. Yet some states like California have become dependent on these dollars, and SLIAG has played a more important role in state fiscal planning than originally expected. While the impact of IRCA and its legalization program has been greatest in California, the long-term implications are national in scope. Congress should therefore evaluate the long-range effects of legalization on federally-funded education and job training programs.

FOOTNOTES

[1] To qualify for permanent resident status, temporary residents had to demonstrate basic citizenship skills in addition to satisfying other requirements. "Basic citizenship skills" are defined in the statute as the ability to "meet the requirements of section 312 (relating to minimal understanding of ordinary English and a knowledge and understanding of the history and government of the United States). . ." or satisfactory pursuit of a recognized course of study designed to achieve such an understanding. IRCA Section 201 (b)(1)(D). Under the implementing regulations, "satisfactory pursuit" could be satisfied if an ELA attended at least 40 hours of a 60-hour program of English and civics instruction and obtained a certificate upon completion of the 40 hours. 8 C.F.R. Section 245a.1(s)(1) and 245a.3(b)(4).

[2] The complete and final report, "Out of the Shadows — The IRCA/SLIAG Opportunity, a Needs Assessment of Educational Services for Eligible Legalized Aliens in California under SLIAG," (Commission Report No. 89-10) is available from the library of the California Postsecondary Education Commission, located at 1020-12th Street, 3rd Floor, Sacramento, California 95814-3985; telephone: (916) 322-8031. Additional information about the substance of the report may be obtained from project director Laurie Olsen at California Tomorrow, Fort Mason Center, Building B, San Francisco, California 94123; telephone: (415) 441-7631.

[3] Phase two describes the process of qualifying and applying for permanent resident status. Phase one refers to the initial process of securing temporary resident status.

[4] The seven critical counties were Monterey, Riverside, San Bernardino, San Mateo, Santa Barbara, Santa Cruz and Stanislaus.

[5] The counties with no capacity problem were Contra Costa, Los Angeles, Orange, San Francisco, Santa Clara, Shasta, Solano, Sonoma, Tulare and Yuba.

[6] H.R. Rep. 682, Part I at 77, 99th Cong., 2d Sess. (1986).

[7] IRCA Section 204 (c)(2)(A) and (B).

[8] IRCA Section 201(h)(4)(G).

Integrating Immigrants into the Labor Market

AARON BODIN

Assistant Commissioner
Immigration and Naturalization Service

There is some small irony in the assigned topic "Integrating Immigrants into the Labor Market," since for many years the Department of Labor (DOL) has been involved in the Alien Labor Certification Program implemented to protect domestic workers from alien competition. Current policy at the Immigration and Naturalization Service (INS), however, comes closer to the mark in that it involves legalizing illegal agricultural workers who have already, to some extent, been integrated into the labor market. A brief status report on the Special Agricultural Worker Program (SAW) and the DOL's plans for the forthcoming Replenishment Agricultural Worker Program (RAW) will be presented.

The passage of IRCA represents a milestone in the long and contentious history of agricultural labor in this country. At long last, the scales are balanced because now employers as well as aliens may be penalized for illegal employment. Recognizing the potentially disruptive effect that sanctions against agricultural employers would have on an industry which had become heavily dependent on illegal labor, Congress provided a two part solution.

In an effort to make it more useable, Congress modified and codified the existing H-2 Program which allows for the temporary admission of foreign workers for specific seasonal jobs on a contract basis. The use of the H-2A Program, as it is now called, has not increased much and it continues to be unpopular with both grower and farmworker advocates — for entirely different reasons, of course.

In the SAW Program, Congress provided for the expansion of the legally available workforce by giving resident status to the foreign workers who had been providing the field labor for perishable crops. The premise of the SAW Program in contrast to the H-2A Program, is that it operates in a free labor market context. In the compromise that broke the deadlock over agricultural workers in the IRCA debate, labor interests insisted that aliens have the freedom to bargain for their labor as legal residents. Because these SAWs would be free to leave agriculture, grower interests insisted that the supply of labor for perishable crops be replenished with additional foreign workers. Thus, the RAW Program was agreed to in which legal resident status would be given to additional foreign workers if the Departments of Labor and Agriculture determined a need for such workers.

The application period for the SAW Program ended this past November. In the words of one commentator, "it was successful beyond our wildest dreams." This was a tongue-in-cheek reference to the fact that the number of applications far exceeded all estimates as to the possible size of the eligible population. Based on USDA estimates, the INS had figured that 500,000 was on the high side of the potentially eligible population and planned for 800,000 applications, three-fourths of which would be filed in the United States.

Experience has been defined as what you get when you are expecting something else; and it has certainly been an experience. Over 1.3 million applications were received — all but 11,000 filed in the United States. This unanticipated workload has caused delays in the process and determinations have been made on only about 30 percent of the applications to date. The approval rate is 93 percent.

It is not likely that the high rate of approval will continue as investigations into possible fraud are completed. The final number of approvals will not be speculated, but a perspective on the fraud will be offered. In recognition of how difficult it would be for illegal aliens to prove the farm work they had done, Congress mandated a very lenient standard of proof. It also required granting employment authorization to applicants and approval of the application, unless the INS could disprove the evidence submitted. It is reasonable that the evidentiary standard should be tolerant given the very informal nature of the farm labor market, and to provide employment authorization to applicants. These policies were effective in providing a largely legal workforce for agriculture in 1988.

What also happened, however, was that a substantial number of aliens who were not farmworkers and were not eligible for the general amnesty program were, because of employer sanctions, in a desperate situation. The law intends that they should leave the country, but many could not resist the temptation to take advantage of the generous standards in the SAW Program to acquire the documentation necessary to obtain employment.

On the bright side, the SAW Program has indeed been a success in that the vast majority of those eligible have applied. They may now work legally and will eventually become permanent residents. The purpose of the law in making the agricultural workforce legally available to growers has, therefore, been achieved. Also, to accomodate traditional patterns of migration, the INS has amended its regulations to allow commuters to live across the border and work in the United States for three to six months every year.

It is now up to agricultural employers to compete in a free market for the services of these workers. I would expect that, in this new environment, wages and working conditions in agriculture will improve. This new environment, of course, includes the vigorous enforcement of employer sanctions in agriculture to which the INS is committed. Neither the need nor the opportunity for the old pattern of illegal employment should exist.

When discussing the admission or adjustment of additional workers under the RAW Program, it should be noted that RAWs, like SAWs, will be legal residents and free to work in any occupation. Also like SAWs, RAWs may remain in the United States or commute to work from a residence across the border. Unlike SAWs, however, to maintain their legal status, they must find work in perishable commodities for 90 days in each of their first three years.

As mentioned, the task of determining the number of RAWs, if any, must be determined jointly by the Departments of Labor and Agriculture. Many will watch with great interest to see how these two agencies will come to agreement on this politically charged question. They must decide on the "shortage number" before each of the four fiscal years during which RAWs may be admitted, beginning this October.

The responsibility of the INS to determine who these RAWs shall be and how they shall be selected, is no less delicate. The INS proposes regulations to govern this process on March 3, and the period for public comment just ended recently.

To be eligible for RAW status, an alien must have been employed in agriculture in the United States for at least twenty days in any twelve month period between May 1, 1985 and November 30, 1988. Priority consideration will be given to persons with this experience who also are the immediate relatives of aliens legalized under IRCA. Unless the shortage number is very large, only eligible aliens residing in the United States will be considered.

The selection process will proceed in two stages. First, eligible aliens will be invited to register their interest in petitioning for RAW status. Then from this pool of registrants, a number equal to the shortage number will be selected at random and invited to petition.

Although by no means unanimous, there appears to be support for these policies in the comments received.

7

The Question of Displaced Persons and the Process of Development in Latin America

AUGUSTO RAMÍREZ-OCAMPO

Assistant Administrator and Regional Director for Latin America and the Caribbean, United Nations Development Programme

It should be established right from the outset that the overall question of immigration and emigration is not the only issue being dealt with here, although at times it becomes difficult to differentiate it from refugee issues. The issue at hand is that of the refugee population, and a new sort of migration which has come to be known as displaced persons.

The question of displaced persons has not represented in the past an international preoccupation, as it has been perceived as a migratory movement within a country's territory, prompted by natural disaster or political upheavals. However, the increasing size of the displaced population in recent years, particularly in Central America, has forced the international community to ask itself to what extent it can continue to ignore a matter which has become a recurrent feature of the situation in affected countries.

Many countries and international organizations are seriously concerned at this time with establishing who should assume a leading responsibility for this population. There are, to be sure, well-defined institutions that deal with immigration, emigration and refugees. Indeed, the United Nations High Commissioner for Refugees (UNHCR) has exercised a mandate in this area since 1951.

However, as regards displaced people, by default the onus may fall upon the United Nations Development Programme (UNDP), although it has not yet been given either the specific mandate or resources to meet the needs of this population. Nonetheless, the international community must rise to the occasion and must ensure the safe transportation of aid and emergency assistance.

This approach has been recently ratified at the International Conference on the Plight of Refugees, Returnees and Displaced Persons in Southern Africa held in Oslo, Norway last August.

It is within this same spirit that the United Nations has organized the Conference for Assistance to Refugees, Displaced Persons and Returnees in Central America for the purpose of defining a program of assistance for these people. This conference is jointly organized by the UN Secretary-General, UNHCR and the UNDP.

There are differences in the manner the needs of refugees and displaced people are attended. Refugees are usually provide temporary humanitarian assistance that is in line with the temporary stay of refugees in other countries. Displaced people, on the other hand, are in need of national plans aiming to their re-incorporation in the normal stream of development in their own countries.

These plans, in turn, must be designed in such a way that they avoid the formation of enclaves or ghettos where living conditions become different from those of the local population.

A balanced policy with respect to local and displaced groups becomes a necessary, if difficult, objective to achieve. The United Nations Secretary-General has asked UNDP to coordinate the United Nations's Special Plan of Economic Co-operation in Central America, in support of the peace process envisioned in the Esquipulas Agreement approved by the General Assembly in May, 1988. In this effort, the UNDP has sought to ensure that the subject of displaced persons receives prominent and immediate attention.

The plan, which seeks to mobilize 4.3 billion dollars over the next three years, has a section dealing distinctly with refugees, displaced population and returnees along with a program of action which covers the five Central American countries and Belize, which has received the impact of migration from El Salvador.

The Special Plan of Economic Co-operation has adopted clear principles, upon which specific assistance will be provided. In this respect, the government of Italy has generously given a donation of the 115 million dollars required to attend to some of the needs of displaced populations in Belize, Costa Rica, El Salvador, Guatemala, Honduras and Nicaragua.

The projects of assistance to the displaced and refugee populations will be carried out, not bilaterally, but under the multilateral aegis of the UN. Accordingly, the Government of Italy, the involved governments of the region and UNDP have agreed that development programs designed for displaced persons will work closely with the populations and the communities themselves, without discrimination, so that they can be the active agents of their own development and are able to assume responsibility for meeting their basic needs and improving their quality of life. The program of assistance to be supported by the government of Italy will benefit 382,400 persons, of which 135,500 will be direct beneficiaries.

The distinctive identity, cultural values and forms of organization chosen by the population must at all times be recognized and respected. Immigrants are admirable people. Dissatisfied with their present conditions, they must relocate within their own countries, or leave them in search of better opportunities even at the risk of confronting the unexpected, stepping, as they do, into the unknown. Refugees who are forced to move from their own environments due to forces beyond their control do not always enjoy the relative freedom of choice of the immigrants.

If the causes of the problem were analyzed, refugees would be found in the misery and backwardness which characterize their living conditions, as well as in the violence, persecution and lack of freedoms that are the facts of their everyday lives.

In a study which was carried out by UNDP at the University of Los Andes in Colombia to look into the causes of migration from the rural areas to the cities, it was found that the first and foremost reason was the search for employment — it should not be forgotten that during the last 30 years Latin America has gone from 70 percent rural and 30 percent urban to a distribution of the population which is exactly the reverse. This flow constitutes the single most massive migratory issue during this entire century.

Cities, even in developing countries, in general offer better living conditions in terms of public services, education, health, social mobility and the potential for personal realization. This explains the difficulty in designing migratory policies which lay emphasis on the causes and not the effects. The underpinnings of the problem are found in a fundamental lack of incentives to remain in the countryside. Any policy that fails to make the rural areas a viable place to live in and work in is a non-policy, and a palliative to the problem.

In the same vein, the most obvious attraction for migrants in the countries of the North can be found in the disparity of development between these countries and those in the South, between the development of the United States and Canada and that of the rest of the countries in the hemisphere. It is sad to realize how a large portion of the selective policies which are applied in the countries of the North, not only aim to attract the best talents but also seek to invite the educated and those with a professional degree who fill an important vacuum in the South such as the sizable "brain drain" of doctors and dentists from Latin America by a country of the North.

Some personal considerations are offered which do not necessarily reflect the opinion of the United Nations and are based on the author's experiences in Latin America as a Parliamentarian, Mayor of Bogota, Minister of Foreign Affairs and university professor.

It bears saying that the United States, which has given rise to the most powerful nation on earth, is a splendid product of a massive immigration prompted by the search for freedom. The United States is in all likelihood the country which has exhibited the greatest generosity in the past by accepting all types of migrants without precluding anybody based on racial, religious or other considerations. The progress and success of the U.S. experiment continue to attract foreigners. The better the economic conditions in this country the more it will continue to act as a magnet for people in developing countries, and particularly by those south of the border.

The most recent statistics in the United States show an unemployment rate of 5.1 percent which for all practical purposes means full employment. In Latin America, unemployment is high and, indeed, it averages 15 percent across the region.

In Central America, there are about 136,000 refugees and close to 1.8 million displaced people, returnees and undocumented persons in a total population of nearly 25 million. These figures are not significantly different from those contained in the "Report of the International Commission for Central American Recovery and Development" which had the central participation of Senator Sanford.

This report gives a figure of 2,271,000 people who are either displaced, returnees or refugees. The Commission's report in fact dramatizes, and rightly so, the magnitude of the problem by indicating that toward 1990 there will be 10 million people below the poverty line in Central America.

Unemployment in Central America is higher than in the rest of Latin America, bordering as it does on some 20 percent of the labor force. Many of these countries have actually regressed and today have per capita incomes equal to or lower than they had 15 years ago. In some cases, such as Nicaragua and El Salvador, per capita income is lower than 30 years ago. In effect, this means that for an entire generation there has been no economic progress.

At a recent meeting of the Inter-American Dialogue, the former Mayor Ferrer of Miami, stated that nearly 500 Nicaraguans are arriving weekly in Miami. Many of them under a new sort of Diaspora which impels them to overcome geographical barriers, crossing the whole of Mexico to become so-called "wetbacks" in California, Arizona, New Mexico and Texas and ending up after a long journey in Florida. Nicaragua is a country with a rate of inflation of nearly 4,400 percent. Who can survive under such a price spiral, compounded by an economic blockade and a drastic reduction in its traditional exports? Under these circumstances, people have no alternative but to emigrate.

The situation in El Salvador is rather similar, although perhaps aggravated by the internal violence of the guerrillas which systematically destroys public wealth. Hondurus has not only absorbed a large number of refugees from El Salvador, but in addition, it now has nearly 11,000 Contras plus their families, which together makes a population of some 30,000 people in a country of just over 4 million. Mexico has also been invaded by refugees in its Yucatan Peninsula and Costa Rica has been burdened with some 200,000 refugees.

The complexity of the subject and the fact that the problems of these seven countries (Belize, Costa Rica, El Salvador, Guatemala, Honduras, Mexico and Nicaragua) are so intertwined that it has made it necessary to approach the subject internationally, multilaterally, multidisciplinarily and multisectorally.

The problem cannot be approached bilaterally: negotiations of this sort are often rife with suspicion, and in any case the absorptive capacity of the United States has limits. Bilateral approaches to the problem hinder global solutions which can only be the real and long-lived ones. For instance, the willingness of some Latin American countries to receive small numbers of Central American refugees has been instrumental, and UNDP is presently designing a prototype cooperation between El Salvador and Bolivia, which might have wider applications in the future.

The unreliability of bilateral solutions to these problems cannot be over-emphasized. It is obvious that Latin America will find it difficult to overcome the lost growth of the last 10 years of its development and to absorb its growing economically active population, which will continue to exert pressure on the countries of the North and particularly on the United States. As long as Latin Americans living in the United States as illegal aliens know that their living conditions here are better than at home, it will be difficult, not to say impossible, to discourage illegal immigration. Moreover, for the country of origin of some of the immigrants, their presence in the United States represents an important source of foreign exchange earnings. For all these, and many more reasons, it is crucial for the United States to give unequivocal support to the process of development in Latin America and, in fact, to do all that is necessary to assist in creating the incentives for such development.

There is a cost-benefit relationship, as outlined:

— The more the United States imposes tariffs and other barriers affecting imports from the Latin American region, such as fruits, flowers, textiles, or products from other labor-intensive industries, the greater the pressure from immigrants will grow.

— The more the United States succumbs to the pressure of internal lobbying to protect inefficient or subsidized local production for goods which compete with those produced in Latin America, the greater the pressure from immigrants will grow.

— The longer it takes to find a rational solution to the debt problem in Latin America, which now amounts to more than 400 billion dollars and has converted the region into a net exporter of capital of 180 billion dollars in the last six years, the greater the pressure from immigrants will grow.

— The more the transfer of technology to support the comparative advantages of Latin American industry is hindered and the more the development of an indigenous industrial capability in the region is hampered, the greater the pressure from immigrants will grow.

In recent years a most tragic paradox has developed: never before has Latin America had so many democratic governments; yet, never before has the continent suffered such regression in its economic development. Today, almost 95 percent of the continent's peoples live under freedom, and democracy — under a pluralism which is based on constitutional traditions. And yet its economic plight threatens the very same political stability and democracy which has been so painstakingly regained.

What is at stake then, is not only the flow of immigrants into the United States, but the survival and well-being of the peoples of Latin America and the sanctity of democracy throughout the hemisphere.

8

Revision of the U.S. Legal System: Toward a Selection System

DORIS M. MEISSNER

Senior Associate, Carnegie Endowment for International Peace

Legislation to change the U.S. system of immigrant selection was enacted by the Senate during its last session and is currently being considered again. (Note: Since delivering these remarks, the Senate enacted S. 358, the Immigration Act of 1989.) Changing legal immigration is a new agenda item for policymakers. Fortunately, the Senate's bill last year did not become law for the changes it contemplated were substantial and poorly understood. To its credit, the Senate immigration subcommittee requested that the General Accounting Office (GAO) do a careful analysis of the bill's longer term ramifications. Its report, presented in recent testimony, is outstanding and should lead to some important modifications in the present bill's draft provisions.

The exercise serves to illustrate, however, the need for care in moving to judgment on legal immigration reforms. The immigrant selection system is complex, and the interplay between the preference system, per country and worldwide ceilings, and nonimmigrant admissions and illegal immigration is subtle and difficult to assess. In addition, the full impact of the legalization program is not yet known, nor is it known how effective employer penalties will be. Until such time as this information is available it is premature and unwise to legislate changes in the current system.

That is not to say that the *status quo* should be maintained. There are clear problems with the present system and reforms will be needed in the years to come. But action should not be precipitous, until the role immigration policy must play in meeting the nation's human resources needs for the 1990s becomes much clearer.

With that in mind, I would like to examine the three key ideas that seem to be underlying the impetus for new legislation. They are: a) family connection immigration is presently too large; b) traditional immigrant-sending nations are discriminated against in the current law; and c) intending immigrants who have skills and labor market attributes the United States needs should have greater access.

FAMILY CONNECTION IMMIGRATION

Family reunification, which has been a sacred tenet of the U.S. immigration system, has been getting a bad name of late. By "bad name," I mean that family-based immigration is now openly denigrated in public debate and commentary in the Congress as producing less skilled and, by implication, less productive immigrants than those who came in earlier years.

This is a new development. Traditionally, politicians have taken extra pains to praise family reunification and the humanitarianism of a system that places heavy emphasis upon this tenet. The shift in attitude is occurring for at least two important reasons.

First, there is research that shows that the education and skills of recent family immigrants are less than that of some earlier groups. Some politicians have taken that to mean that these immigrants are not contributing as their forebears did.

Secondly, the manner in which chain migration strains the immigration preference system is becoming an increasing concern. Queues of many years' duration raise questions about the basic workability of the system. In addition, chain immigration consists, naturally, of the same nationality groups that dominate overall immigration flows. Thus, family immigration is also viewed as contributing to the lack of substantial national diversity in U.S. immigrant admissions.

Family immigration is the "centerpiece" of U.S. immigration policy and has been so historically. The reason is not simply sentimentality. Nor is it a concession to particular immigrant groups, who claim that the extended family is a more enduring characteristic of their cultures.

The reason is that family groups in immigrant communities function as the source of stability — social and economic — for newcomers coming into the country. The family provides the primary mechanism through which resettlement and adaptation to a new society occurs. Without it, an elaborate social services system to provide labor market information and intermediaries with the host culture would be needed for immigration policy to work. This must be clearly described, understood and appreciated by policymakers as they consider changes in the immigrant selection system. Family immigration does not deserve a bad name; instead, its importance and function needs to be more fully grasped by decisionmakers.

At the same time, concerns about the sweep of chain migration are legitimate and constitute a real political and substantive issue in the debate. The concerns center on the second (immediate relatives of lawful permanent residents) and fifth (siblings) preferences. For example, the visa queues from countries such as Mexico and the Philippines are now so many years long that the favored treatment intended by the structure of preferences serves as not much more than a symbol, instead of a viable mechanism for family union.

Furthermore, queues of five to ten years' duration and more are so unrealistic, from the point of view of individual intending immigrants' decisions, that they all but encourage illegal immigration, because the incentive to play by the rules is not likely to produce results in any reasonable time period.

Some willingness to address the problem of chain migration is essential. The formula that best preserves a family-based system is one that allows the spouses and children of both lawful permanent residents and citizens to immigrate without regard to numerical limits, but also to limit the fifth preference to unmarried siblings.

This would mean that family reunification would be certain for immediate family members of new immigrants and citizens alike, regardless of country of origin. As a result, the central objective of the U.S. immigration system would be a real one. By limiting preference for siblings to those who are not married, the number of people with claims on the system would be relatively finite. It is according preference to married siblings that leads to the chain effect and to queues that can never realistically be served.

Such a change would not, however, eliminate a preferred status for married sibling immigration as those who oppose it fear. If independent, skills-based immigration is increased, as all present proposals contemplate, siblings will compete for those slots more effectively than most any other group of aspiring immigrants. This is because they will have superior labor market information and potential jobs to rely upon, based on family connections already in the country.

The best evidence of this assertion comes from Canada and Australia. Both have a significant proportion of their immigrant selection based on skills criteria and find that substantial numbers of those selected through such criteria turn out, also, to have family already in their countries. Despite what is sometimes believed, those who wish to come to the United States and to other immigration countries are by and large people who have established connections with the United States either through family, educational experience or relevant work experience. If the system opens up access to more independent immigration, siblings are likely to gain access to immigrant visas that is at least as great, and perhaps greater, than they do with the current fifth preference.

TRADITIONAL IMMIGRANT-SENDING NATIONS

Today, nine nations account for about half of U.S. immigrants. They are all
in Asia or Latin America. This is a dramatic change from the pattern that has
existed throughout U.S. history, when the vast majority of immigrants came
from Europe. The shift has given rise to a sense that the 1965 amendments to
the Immigration and Nationality Act that eliminated a discriminatory immigrant selection system, based upon national origins quotas, has had the
unintended consequence of discriminating against immigration from Europe.

Some argue, therefore, that the law should be changed to assure greater
diversity among sending nations. This is a noble principle, but no one has
yet fashioned a formula to achieve it that does not reintroduce a bias into the
selection process that would favor some nations or parts of the world; *i.e.,*
another form of national origins discrimination. In frustration, the Congress
has now twice authorized visa lotteries in an attempt to respond to the
political pressure surrounding this issue. In the most recent, the first three
countries from whom "winners" were chosen were Pakistan, Iran and Ku-
wait. These are not at all what proponents had in mind. However, they show
the folly of trying to engineer particular nationality results in the selection
system.

The reason traditional sending nations seem to be losing out is because
they no longer have qualifying family connection immigrants in the United
States. Once close relatives have arrived or, with the passage of time, are no
longer alive, the basis for immigrant eligibility disappears. Thus, the law does
not discriminate against particular countries. Instead, in disproportionately
favoring family reunion, it all but precludes immigration for any but those
from countries where recent immigrant flows exist.

The way to fix the problem is not to reintroduce nationality bias into the
law. It is, instead, to provide for larger numbers of independent immigrants
to qualify for admission. Presently, less than 10 percent of U.S. immigrant
slots (third and sixth preferences) are available for nonfamily immigrants. If
these preferences become the focus of debate and action, both through
increased numbers and possible redefinition, the system will contain the
needed mechanism to allow greater access to those without family links and,
in turn, greater sending-nation diversity. This assumes people from traditional source countries wish to settle in the United States.

INCREASED INDEPENDENT IMMIGRATION

The recommendations of the Select Commission on Immigration and Refugee
Policy (SCIRP), delivered in 1981, called for changes in the way the nation
manages both illegal and legal immigration. Indeed, the legislation that was

introduced in the early 1980s to introduce employer penalties also included substantial revisions of the legal immigration system that would provide increased access for nonfamily connection immigrants with skills and occupations useful to the United States.

Those changes were ultimately dropped in the interests of enacting legislation to diminish illegal immigration. But the sponsors, Senators Kennedy and Simpson in particular, continued to speak of the need to enact reforms to the immigrant selection system as the next agenda item.

They have kept their promise, and are sponsoring legislation that would significantly increase the numbers of independent immigrants and introduce a point system for selecting them.

Independent immigration should be increased but the mechanism should be by working with the third and sixth preferences of the current system, rather than by introducing a point system. That is to say, the present system provides for the admission of people with occupations and labor market attributes, of interest to the United States, through the preference system. The problem is that it allocates such a small proportion of the available annual slots to them that less than 10 percent of U.S. legal immigration is granted on this basis. This could be readily solved by increasing the proportion of immigrants admitted through the occupational preferences and/or the overall level of immigration from the current 270,000 annual ceiling.

Moreover, the current system has the advantage of being responsive to particular labor market needs because it vests employers with the opportunity to request particular individuals, based on their occupational qualifications, if American workers will not be adversely affected. The labor certification process, has proven unwieldy over the years and does not enjoy much support within the employer community nor in the Congress. Nonetheless, were it overhauled, it is a more effective way of structuring immigrant selection than a point system would be. Point systems work very well in Australia and Canada, nations that have used them for years and that constitute the other major immigrant receiving nations in the world. The difficulty that the method poses for the United States, in contrast, is that both Australia and Canada have parliamentary systems of government. That means that their point systems, while authorized in law, are established and modified on a regular basis by their immigration ministries, the equivalent of the U.S. executive branch. The reason they work well is because they are flexible tools that can be and are altered to respond to the changing needs of the nation and changes in the applicant populations.

The system that is being proposed for the United States is one that would be fixed in law and therefore extremely difficult to modify. Flexibility is the key to the workability of a point system. If the United States were to adopt one, it would do what is least needed; that is, introduce another layer of rigidity to an already regulation-bound, inflexible system.

Existing research and analysis show that the United States is likely to experience tight labor markets in the decade ahead. One response to that eventuality is to conclude that the possibility of labor shortages can be sidestepped by increased immigration. On the other hand, it is only when the labor market is tight that employers and the larger society find ways — generally through training, restructuring work and raising wages — to reach into the ranks of the under- and unemployed and make them productive workers. Doing this has widespread implications not only for employment policy but for attacking a range of larger social policy quandaries that can only be resolved if people are working at jobs that pay decent wages.

Before acting upon the assumption that the possibility of a tight labor market should lead to significantly increased immigration and a point system to select people, the tradeoffs need to be examined and the appropriate balance struck. The approach I favor is to work with today's occupational preferences as the basis for reform at the moment and to devote a great deal more attention to understanding how immigration policy might advance the larger human resources interests of the nation in the 1990s, before enacting sweeping changes to the U.S. immigrant selection system.

9

Proposed Bush Administration
Legal Immigration Reform Plan

RICHARD E. NORTON
Associate Commissioner
Immigration and Naturalization Service

In the first year of the new Administration, the effort begun by the old Administration in 1981 regarding immigration should be completed. A major legislative initiative to review and improve the U.S. system of legal immigration should now be pursued.

On November 6, 1986, President Reagan signed into law the sweeping Immigration Reform and Control Act (IRCA). This legislation provided an opportunity for millions of previously illegal aliens to become legal members of U.S. society. It also significantly enhanced the ability of the United States to regain control of its own borders, to prevent illegal aliens from entering the American job market, to combat abuses of the entitlement programs by aliens and to deal effectively with criminal aliens in the United States. One of the most important sections of IRCA provided for sanctions to be levied against employers who intentionally hire aliens who are not authorized to work in the United States. As important and as necessary as these provisions are in dealing with the problem of illegal aliens, they do not address the other side of the equation relating to legal immigration.

The Bush Administration now has a unique opportunity to sponsor legislation addressing the problems contained in the current immigration statutes. How this country handles immigration matters may be determined for decades to come to ensure that the immigration policies of the United States support such cherished ideals as promoting family unity and revitalizing the American economy.

The timing is right. Immigration remains a solid bi-partisan issue. It would be an excellent accomplishment and demonstration of good government of the Administration and Congress to achieve legal immigration reform in 1989. Several goals have been outlined:

1) anticipate and meet future labor demands of U.S. employers;
2) significantly reduce or eliminate backlogs of people waiting to come to the United States;
3) encourage immigrating aliens to become citizens of the United States; and
4) assure that legal immigration takes the place of illegal immigration.

BROAD THEMES

— The current immigration law places a severe burden on the nuclear family, in some cases preventing reunification for up to ten years and fostering illegal immigration. The proposed legislation assures that family members are quickly reunited.

— The current law often fails to meet the immediate needs of individual American employers or to encourage investment in the American economy. While still emphasizing the nuclear family, the proposed legislation addresses the needs of the American economy by facilitating the entry of needed workers and investors.

— The current law places annual restrictions on the number of aliens who may immigrate from any one country in any preference category, resulting in some families being separated for extended periods of time and some American companies not obtaining critically needed employees. The proposed legislation eliminates these per-country restrictions for all family reunification and most professional or occupational categories.

— The current law allows only those with close family ties or specific offers of employment to enter the United States as immigrants. The proposed legislation creates opportunities for others who have the initiative and desire to live in and contribute to the American system.

— The current law contains no provisions to address the changing needs of American society. The proposed legislation provides a mechanism whereby the executive and legislative branches of government can easily review and make changes to the immigration process on a regular basis.

— The current law's five year residency requirement to become a citizen adversely affects the backlog in immigration and delays the reunification of families. The proposed law reduces the required residency period to three years in order to promote family reunification. At the same time, the proposed legislation retains the high standards and traditional ceremonial aspects of the citizenship process.

— The proposed law strengthens the U.S. heritage of legal immigration by keeping the entry numbers at a high level and actually making some increases (to the range of 600,000 to 700,000 immigrants annually). Illegal immigration levels, which should be reduced under IRCA, will be a factor in setting levels, thereby promoting a system of legal immigration.

PROJECTED FLOW

The plan provides for four major categories of immigration:

1) Immediate Relative. The spouse, children or parents of a citizen of the United States.

2) Family Reunification. Those who are joining relatives who are lawful permanent residents instead of citizens.

3) Occupational Preference. Those whose services are sought by U.S. employers or who are investing substantial amounts of capital in employment-creating enterprises in the United States.

4) Independent Selection. Those who have the potential to contribute to the economy and to assimilate into U.S. society, but do not have a qualifying relative or employer to serve as a sponsor.

Overall levels of immigration would rise for several years but would eliminate current delays in the immigration process and would permit the immigration of dependents of aliens who became legalized under the Immigration Reform and Control Act of 1986.

PROVISIONS

The proposed legislation would encourage immigrating aliens to become citizens of the United States through the naturalization process by:

1) reducing the required residency period from five years to three years, without lowering the standards relating to the alien's knowledge of American history and government or attachment to the principles of our constitution; and

2) facilitating the process by which citizens bring relatives to the United States, while de-emphasizing the same process for those aliens who choose not to make a commitment to the United States by becoming citizens. The ability to petition for relatives to immigrate to the United States is already the driving factor in the decision of most aliens to seek United States citizenship. The proposed plan would greatly enhance this factor in that the petition process would not be available after three years to those who choose not to become citizens.

The Immediate Relative category would be retained as under the current law, but would contain an added item for the dependent children of immediate relatives in order to prevent family separation. The reduction in the required residency period for citizenship from five to three years would enable people to bring such relatives to the United States sooner.

The Family Reunification category would initially provide sufficient visa numbers to take care of current demand, existing backlogs, and new immigration pressure created by the legalization program. Fifty thousand visas would be allocated for the never-married sons and daughters of citizens. One hundred and fifty thousand would go to the spouses and never-married children of lawful permanent residents. This category would sunset after three years, replaced by an expanded definition of "following to join" which provides for visa issuance to qualifying spouses, sons and daughters, regardless of whether the qualifying relationship existed at the time of the immigrant alien's entry as a permanent resident, provided application is made within three years of such entry. An extra 50,000 visas would be available each year for the ten years after enactment to eliminate the existing backlog of spouses and children of permanent residents waiting to immigrate. Further growth of backlogs in this category would be stopped by the provision of up to 50,000 visas annually through December 31, 1991 for the spouse and children of legalized aliens.

The Occupational Preference category would provide visas for up to 125,000 aliens who possess skills needed by U.S. employers. Persons immigrating under this category would be required to remain in the same occupational field (but not necessarily with the same employer) for three years. Twenty thousand visas would be available to doctoral professionals whose services are sought by U.S. employers. Fifty thousand professionals with baccalaureate degrees (or the equivalent) could enter if they are sought by employers who cannot find qualified workers in the United States. Another 50,000 visas would be set aside for other skilled immigrants whose services are needed by employers. Visa numbers not used by the first three occupational preference subcategories would be allocated to unskilled workers with valid certifications. The remaining 5,000 visas would be allocated for people investing at least 1,000,000 dollars in an enterprise which creates employment opportunities for Americans.

The Independent Selection category would provide a new source of immigrants whose attributes include U.S. citizen relatives, desirable talents and the skills required for rapid adjustment to residence in the United States. One hundred thousand visas would be provided for those scoring the most points based on the following scale:[1]

1) The married son or daughter or the brother or sister of a United

States citizen who is the beneficiary of a visa petition filed under the prior law (sunsets in 3 years) (30 points).

2) The married son or daughter or the brother or sister of a United States citizen (20 points).

3) The native of a country which is underrepresented in immigration to the U.S., compared to either its traditional level of immigration or its percentage of world population (10 points).

4) Persons possessing either training or experience in occupations which are in demand in the United States (10-30 points).

5a) Persons having arranged employment in an occupation qualifying under item 4 (20 points).

5b) Persons having other arranged employment, except in certain fields with high unemployment levels (10 points).

6) Persons who are fluent in English (10 points).

7) Persons with baccalaureate degrees (10 points).

8a) Persons 18-35 years old (10 points).

8b) Persons 36-45 years old (5 points).

The law would be streamlined by substituting the above provisions (items 1 and 2) for the current fourth preference (relating to married sons and daughters of citizens) and the current fifth preference (relating to brothers and sisters of citizens).

The current limitation of no more than 20,000 visas for any one country per year would be stricken for all categories except for the 100,000 visas for baccalaureate-level professionals, skilled workers and unskilled workers.

Miscellaneous provisions would:

1) provide for consultation between the Executive and Legislative branches of government every three years or when total immigration exceeds 650,000 persons annually; levels of illegal immigration will be considered in such consultations;

2) create specific provisions for recovering funds from sponsors if a sponsored immigrant receives welfare payments;

3) require continuation of judicial naturalization in place of proposals for an administrative naturalization system; and

4) eliminate inordinate delays in the immigration of immediate family members.

FOOTNOTE

[1] The points for the independent category are intended as an example; they may be modified during the review process.

10

Reforming the Criteria for the Exclusion and the Deportation of Alien Criminal Offenders

STEPHEN H. LEGOMSKY

Washington University

My subject is the exclusion and the deportation of those aliens who have committed crimes. Having taught immigration law now for several years, I have fallen into the habit of introducing this material on alien criminal offenders by posing the following hypothetical: Two aliens arrive at the United States border on exactly the same day. Both are lawfully admitted for permanent residence. Five years go by. Alien #1 goes out and commits a premeditated murder. The same day, alien #2 is found in possession of a joint of marijuana. Both aliens eventually are convicted of their respective crimes. Students are asked which of these aliens, if either, is deportable. And with the text of the Immigration and Nationality Act laid out in front of them, they discover, consistently to their amazement, that the marijuana possessor is deportable while the murderer, at least until extremely recently, was not.

The reason for this combination of results is that an alien who has been convicted of a crime involving what the statute calls "moral turpitude" is deportable, but only if that crime was committed during the first five years after entry.[1] In contrast, an alien who has been convicted of a drug offense is deportable regardless of when the crime was committed.[2]

I cannot use that precise hypothetical any more because Congress changed the law this past November. It passed the Anti-Drug Abuse Act of 1988.[3] The Act is quite sweeping, but one particular provision creates a new category of offenses called "aggravated felonies."[4] These are defined as murder, drug trafficking, and trafficking in firearms or destructive devices.[5] Under this

law, classifying a crime as an aggravated felony has several legal consequences, one is that, if the offender is an alien, the conviction will render the
person deportable without regard to the five-year limit otherwise applicable
to crimes involving moral turpitude.[6] So today the correct answer to my
hypothetical question would be that the murderer is deportable too.

But the basic anomaly still exists, and I can still salvage most of the
hypothetical by substituting some other serious crime for murder. That is not
hard to do. The rapist, the armed robber, the kidnapper, the arsonist, the
person who assaults another with a deadly weapon or who assaults another
with the intent to kill — none of these people is deportable under the present
law as long as he or she waits until at least five years after entry to commit
the crime. The marijuana possessor, in contrast, is deportable whether that
person has lived in the United States lawfully for one day or thirty years.

In order not to mislead, I should mention that there do exist two waiver
provisions applicable specifically to marijuana offenders: one statutory provision and one internal INS Operations Instruction.[7,8] The eligibility rules
under both provisions are quite limited, however, and in addition, even for
those aliens who meet the qualifying requirements, the ultimate grant of
relief requires the favorable exercise of administrative discretion. So the
current laws do treat even marijuana offenders, and certainly other drug
offenders, much more harshly than they treat those aliens who have been
convicted of crimes involving moral turpitude.

There are other anomalies as well. I'll spell out just a few. Even if an alien
commits a crime involving moral turpitude during the first five years, deportation still cannot take place unless he or she is sentenced to at least a year of
confinement.[9] There is no analogous requirement for drug offenses.[10] The
sentencing judge in a drug case, after hearing all the evidence, could find the
particular offense trivial enough to warrant sentencing the alien to nothing
more than a fine, but under the immigration laws that would not matter. The
alien will be deportable regardless of the sentence imposed and, again,
regardless of how many years or even decades the person has lived a lawful
existence in the United States.

Similarly, a Presidential or gubernatorial pardon erases the conviction of
a crime involving moral turpitude for deportation purposes.[11] A pardon does
not wipe out a drug conviction for that purpose.[12] Again, and more important
than the pardon example in terms of volume, if an alien has been convicted
of a crime involving moral turpitude, the sentencing judge has the statutory
power to block any deportation that would have been based on that conviction, simply by issuing a binding recommendation to that effect.[13] The same
statutory provision expressly forbids the sentencing judge from doing so in
the case of a drug offense.[14]

All those examples concern deportation. There are similar anomalies on the exclusion side of the ledger. Both the alien who has been convicted of a crime involving moral turpitude and the alien convicted of a drug crime are generally inadmissible.[15] In the case of the moral turpitude crime, however, the statute lays out several exceptions. For example, if the crime was committed while the alien was under eighteen and it was more than five years ago, the statute waives the exclusion ground automatically.[16] There is no comparable exception for drug crimes. Along the same lines, if an alien who is convicted of a crime involving moral turpitude receives a sentence of less than six months, then again the corresponding exclusion ground is waived automatically and again there is no comparable exception for drug offenses.[17]

Further examples could be offered, but those discussed are enough to make clear that the patterns I have described are not accidental. They represent a deliberate course of action on the part of Congress. Over the years Congress has been quite consistent in treating even the mildest drug offenses more harshly, for immigration purposes, than some of the most vicious offenses that do not involve drugs.

In making that point, I hope I am not misunderstood. I don't want to trivialize the paralyzing effects of drug abuse. As a father, I would be the last person to suggest that the government be anything less than zealous both in attacking the root causes of drug abuse and in responding to its immediate consequences. At the same time, some perspective must be maintained. It simply cannot be true that the alien who is arrested for smoking a joint is a greater menace to our society than the rapist or the arsonist or the armed robber or the person who assaults another with a deadly weapon. Yet that is precisely the premise on which our current immigration laws rest.

This is an area in which judicial reform is destined to be ineffectual. A case called *Lieggi* v. *United States INS* shows why.[18] Lieggi was an alien who had immigrated from Italy to the United States as a small child with his family, and who as an adult was convicted of having sold three marijuana cigarettes to his former roommate. The INS, with all the love and compassion for which it has become famous, instituted deportation proceedings. It alleged that Lieggi was deportable by virtue of his conviction of a drug offense, which he was. The federal district court enjoined the deportation order. It reasoned that, given the mildness of the offense on the one hand and the severity of the resulting sanction on the other hand, deporting Lieggi would be cruel and unusual punishment.

But the district court was bucking the previously unbroken rule that deportation, however cruel and unusual it might well be on a given set of facts, was technically not punishment. Therefore the constitutional prohibition of cruel and unusual punishment simply did not apply to deportation.

Consequently, the Court of Appeals for the Seventh Circuit quickly reversed.[19]

So if reform is to come, it will have to come from Congress. Precisely what the changes should be is certainly a matter on which reasonable minds can disagree. That is the hard question, and I admit I have ducked it thus far. I would simply say this. Once it is accepted that the present disparities between drug offenses and more turpitude offenses are indeed anomalous, and my view is that they are, then there are, of course, at least two ways in which to proceed — either liberalize the drug provisions or toughen the moral turpitude provisions. Which course one thinks preferable is dictated more by personal values than by logic. The former option, admittedly unlikely in the present political climate, is one I personally find more palatable.

My view rests on two premises. First, to state the obvious, the stakes for the individual are enormous. Realistically, the aliens most affected by the present disparities are lawfully admitted permanent residents. Aliens here illegally are already deportable even without the criminal provisions. Aliens here lawfully as nonimmigrants can be affected, but the vast bulk of them have been here less than five years, so the time differential between drug offenses and other offenses would not usually matter. The main concern, therefore, is permanent resident aliens — those individuals who stand to lose home, family, job, and lifestyle.

Secondly, the aliens in question have already been punished by the criminal law. These are aliens who have already paid their debts to society. It seems fair to assume that the existing range of criminal sentences reflects the legislative judgment as to what level of punishment is commensurate with each crime; exclusion and deportation are *additional* sanctions.

The patterns discussed and the discrepancies those patterns reveal are just one small part of a much broader inquiry: What, exactly, should the criteria be for determining whether an alien who has been convicted of a crime should be excluded, or should be deported? Should the phrase "moral turpitude," with its inherent vagueness, be a criterion at all? David Martin and his co-author Alex Aleinikoff, in their excellent casebook, have demonstrated convincingly that there are some real problems with the phrase "moral turpitude."[20] I believe plausible alternatives exist and will set forth some preliminary thoughts on how the law might be recast.

On the assumption that the central objectives of both exclusion and deportation are to rid the country of those aliens whose admission or continued presence would be socially harmful, the two most obvious criteria for determining whether a criminal conviction should trigger either exclusion or deportation are the number of crimes and the degree of social harm reflected in those crimes. In the case of deportation, it seems logical to consider also the length of time the alien has lived in the United States; the societal benefits of expulsion can thus be at least crudely balanced against the disruption to the life of the individual alien. To varying degrees, these general principles are already reflected in current laws.

Putting all this together, I would scrap the moral turpitude test entirely, and would also eliminate the various provisions that single out drug offenses for unique treatment. I would substitute a single provision or set of provisions that lay out several combinations of the two (for exclusion) or three (for deportation) variables just described: number of crimes committed, the sentences for those crimes, and, in deportation cases, the length of time the person has been in the United States at the moment deportation proceedings are instituted. This last factor is a statute of limitations; it differs from the present time limits, which are measured by the interval between the alien's entry and the commission of the crime.[21] The time elapsed between entry and institution of deportation proceedings seems preferable because that period is more likely to reflect the depth of the person's roots.

The reason I focus on sentence is that it is as accurate a vehicle as any for gauging the seriousness of the crime. A sentence test seems better than attempting in advance to identify all the offenses that would trigger exclusion or deportation, and better than trying in individual cases to figure out what a phrase like "moral turpitude" or "serious" or "grave" means in practical terms. To be sure, the accumulated case law now furnishes voluminous examples of crimes that do, and crimes that do not, involve moral turpitude. But the process has been painful, and, even given the judicial work that has been done up to now, every new criminal offense in every jurisdiction creates a new and unnecessary immigration law issue.

Still, other policy decisions will have to be made if sentence becomes a statutory criterion: should the test be the maximum sentence that could be imposed under the particular statute, or should it be the punishment actually imposed in the individual case? The sentence imposed would reflect the opinion of the sentencing judge, who saw and heard the evidence in the case firsthand and thus can reflect in the sentence the defendant's actual degree of moral culpability. On the negative side, though, going by the sentence imposed means that deportation could hinge on whether the particular sentencing judge was tough or lax. A third possibility is to go by time actually served, a possibility that presents a similar tradeoff. The parole board can take even more individual behavior into account; it can consider post-conviction behavior. Again, the drawback is that deportation would then hinge on the vagaries of the particular parole board. So choosing among these alternatives presents a real tension between the goal of basing the deportation decision on maximum information about the individual and the goal of equal treatment.

In conclusion, the current provisions governing the treatment of alien criminal offenders seem impossible to defend rationally. The discrepancies between drug crimes and other crimes is a significant part of the problem, and the use of a phrase as vague as "moral turpitude" is another large part. I urge Congress to wipe the slate clean and to rewrite this entire set of provisions from scratch.

FOOTNOTES

[1] Immigration and Nationality Act [hereafter INA] §241(a)(4)(A), 8 U.S.C. §1251(a)(4)(A).

[2] INA §241(a)(11), 8 U.S.C. §1251(a)(11).

[3] Pub. L. 100-690, 102 Stat. 4181, 100th Cong., 2d Sess. (Nov. 18, 1988).

[4] *Id.* §7342, adding INA §101(a)(43), 8 U.S.C. §1101(a)(43).

[5] *Id.*

[6] *See* INA §241(a)(4)(B), 8 U.S.C. §1251(a)(4)(B).

[7] INA §241(f)(2), 8 U.S.C. §1251(f)(2).

[8] INS Operations Instruction 242.1(a)(26).

[9] INA §241(a)(4)(A), 8 U.S.C. §1251(a)(4)(A).

[10] INA §241(a)(11), 8 U.S.C. §1251(a)(11).

[11] INA §241(b)(1), 8 U.S.C. §1251(b)(1).

[12] Section 241(b) is expressly limited to deportations based on section 241(a)(4), the moral turpitude provision. To remove any possible doubt, Congress added a sentence making section 241(b) expressly inapplicable to deportations based on section 241(a)(11), the drug provision.

[13] INA §241(b)(2), 8 U.S.C. §1251(b)(2).

[14] *See supra* note 12.

[15] INA §212(a)(9,23), 8 U.S.C. §1182(a)(9,23).

[16] INA §212(a)(9), 8 U.S.C. §1251(a)(9).

[17] *Id.*

[18] 389 F.Supp. 12 (N.D. Ill. 1975).

[19] *See* 529 F.2d 530 (7th Cir. 1976) (unpublished decision).

[20] T. Aleinikoff & D. Martin, *Immigration: Process and Policy.* 1985:377-398.

[21] For a more detailed discussion of the differences, *see id.* at 369-72.

11

The Unfinished Business of Immigration Reform

Legislative Analyst, American Civil Liberties Union

The task of revising the McCarran-Walter Act grounds for excluding and deporting foreigners from the United States was, as most are likely aware, set aside from the legislative undertaking of rewriting the immigration laws in the Simpson-Rodino package.

It had long been the common wisdom that Congress — especially in an election year — was not prepared to repeal this McCarthy era law barring communists and others affiliated with suspect ideologies from visiting or residing in the United States. One senator recently reflected the general sentiment about this particular problem, "The less said about it, the better."

But, "the times, they are a changin'." There is a growing consensus that the ideological exclusion provisions of the McCarran-Walter Act are embarassing, inappropriate, anachronistic, decidedly ineffective in safe-guarding our security needs and contrary to at least the spirit of the first amendment. In fact, the Supreme Court has recognized the First Amendment interest at stake for Americans who have been denied their right to meet with foreigners in this country and the litigation of visa denials has been based on that predicate.

The effort to repeal this law has been given an unintended assist by the State Department. For example: In 1985, Farley Mowat, a Canadian nature writer, was prohibited from entering the United States to make a promotional trip for a recent book because of his past statements and affiliations.

In 1983, Mrs. Hortensia Allende, the widow of the former President of Chile, was denied a visa to speak in the United States about women and human rights issues because the State Department determined that her speech activities would be prejudicial to the public interest. This denial was challenged, and the First Circuit Court of Appeals held the denial invalid on several grounds. First, the Court found that the State Department had attempted to circumvent a 1978 amendment to the McCarran-Walter Act intended to provide a presumptive waiver for foreigners excludable on the grounds of affiliation. Secondly, the Court held that the provision of the Act allowing for visa denials based on activities in the U.S. prejudicial to the public interest did not include the foreign policy consequences of a foreigner's mere entry of presence in the United States. The court also noted that a 1987 amendment prohibited the government from issuing Mrs. Allende a visa because of her "past, current or expected beliefs, statements or associations."

It is true that the Congress has yet to repeal the McCarran-Walter Act. It is also true that there are concrete signs of progress in that direction.

In 1987, the Congress passed the Amendment, just referred to, as part of the State Department Authorization Bill. It is known to its friends as "Section 901." In 1988, the Congress extended what had initially been a one-year provision for another two years. Section 901 is a clear statement of the consensus position of the Congress — that beliefs, statements or associations are proscribed grounds for making visa determinations. The new law, however, has some troubling exceptions. In addition, it did not repeal the underlying McCarran-Walter Act and thus the State Department continues to ask foreigners if they "are now or have ever been" communists, etc., and then to determine whether or not a waiver is appropriate.

Section 901 is an indication that the Congress is moving on this issue. In that instance, it moved thanks to the impetus provided by Senators Moynihan, Kassebaum and Simon. The lead and longstanding champion of the effort to revise the exclusion and deportation provisions of the McCarran-Walter Act is, of course, Barney Frank.

At the last three congressional sessions, Congressman Frank has introduced legislation that would entirely revamp the McCarran-Walter Act. Last year, his bill made it through the full Judiciary Committee. This year, the new Immigration Subcommittee chair, Bruce Morrison, is committed to moving that bill through the subcommittee in the coming months. Hopefully, the full committee will also make this effort a priority.

Congressman Frank's bill would repeal all of the ideological provisions of current law and in its place provide for the exclusion of foreigners who would be likely to violate the laws of the United States after entry or who had previously engaged in acts of terrorism. The bill also provides narrow and specific instances in which, for foreign policy reasons, the State Department would be authorized to deny admission.

The ACLU supports this bill and hopes that the bill will move swiftly through the House of Representatives, and that the Senate will follow suit. Indeed, we are optimistic that at long last, with some urging, the 101st Congress will finally remove this law from the books. In the words of Nobel Prize winning novelist Carlos Fuentes, a self-described past and future victim of the McCarran-Walter Act:

> . . .it is your law and it is you, out of sheer self-respect, sheer self-interest, sheer self-consciousness of what you are and represent that must change it. It is a law that hurts me and other foreign individuals. But the real, the permanent, the long-range victim of this law is the United States of America.

PART IV
REFUGEES: INTERNATIONAL PERSPECTIVES AND DOMESTIC POLICY ISSUES

12

Selected Issues in Soviet Jewish Migration

JUDITH E. GOLUB
American Jewish Committee

Soviet Jews hold a central place emotionally, spiritually and politically in the hearts and minds of the American Jewish community. A large number of American Jews are either first or second generation descendants of Russian Jews or have family members still living in the Soviet Union. Many have followed with much concern the lives of Soviet Jews living in the USSR as a persecuted minority and how Soviet policy has impacted on Jewish life and emigration rates. Many also have, not only watched, but worked actively both in the nation's capital and in their local communities in support of increased emigration rates and lobbied on behalf of a specific "refusenik" who had been denied exit permission by the Soviet government. Such denials often resulted from such contrived charges as possession of state secrets and the "poor relative" loophole, which prohibits potential emigrants from leaving if their departure supposedly would cause economic hardship for those left behind.

In the mid-sixties, Soviet Jews began to press for the right to emigrate, asserting that the Universal Declaration of Human Rights and other international accords to which the USSR had subscribed gave them the right to leave their country. At that time, virtually all opted to go to Israel, with only a few choosing to join family members already in the United States. However, after the 1973 Yom Kippur War, many changed their minds about their final destination, and, upon reaching Vienna, declared their intention to proceed to the United States instead of Israel. They came to this country as refugees and, as such, were entitled to federal aid for transportation and resettlement, and were permitted to seek citizenship. To be deemed a refugee, according to the Refugee Act of 1980, applicants had to satisfy several criteria:

— meet the definition of refugee which was mandated in the Immigration and Nationality Act; that is, establish a "well-founded fear of persecution" on account of race, nationality, religion, membership in a particular social group or political opinion;

— be of special humanitarian concern to the United States;

— be otherwise admissible under U.S. law; and

— not be firmly resettled in any foreign country.

The numbers of Soviet Jews allowed to emigrate has changed dramatically over time. To a large extent, emigration rates have correlated with the ups and downs of Soviet-American relations. Small numbers of Soviet Jews entered the U.S. prior to 1973, preceding larger numbers who came in the late 1970s and early 1980s. However, a deterioration of relations in the early part of this decade caused emigration rates to slow to a trickle by the mid-1980s.

Currently, however, much seems to have changed. President Mikhail Gorbachev is allowing thousands of Jews to leave the Soviet Union. In fact, from January to the end of November 1989, an unprecedented 67,000 have been allowed to leave. However, numerical and budgetary limitations imposed by both the Administration and Congress, have led the U.S. government to seek to cope with this unexpected influx in novel ways. To the surprise and disappointment of many, significant numbers of Soviet Jews in both Moscow and Rome (the final European destination for those who decide in Vienna to apply to enter the U.S. and where they await determination of their refugee status) have been denied refugee status, even though they had been granted permission to leave the Soviet Union.

Those denied entry as refugees have been offered parole, an authority under which, in special circumstances, the Attorney General of the United States may admit individuals in dangerous circumstances who are not granted entry expeditiously under existing law. By statute, parole may not be granted to refugees except under rare and special circumstances. Once they arrive in the U.S., paroles are ineligible for federal aid and may adjust to permanent resident status only with great difficulty. However, recent legislation, briefly reviewed below, mandates this adjustment.

Shortly after the Soviet emigration gates began to open in late 1988, the U.S. government appeared to change its refugee policies. By denying refugee status to an unprecedented number of Jews in Moscow (about 46%) and in Rome (about 20%), the government seemed to be signaling both a dramatic shift in its view of Soviet Jews as a persecuted minority and an about-face in this country's political will. (Importantly, of those cases in Rome appealing their denial, about 60% have been overturned.) These denials mark the first time that the U.S. has refused refugee status to a significant number of Soviet Jews.

The U.S. government has responded to these assertions by stating that it has not changed its policies toward Soviet Jews but, in an effort to apply immigration laws more uniformly, can no longer be as lenient as it had in the past. Others view the situation differently, asserting that the government has changed its policies mid-stream and that these denials are the direct result of a budget deficit which has led to sharp cuts in every agency of the federal government. Still others assert that increased and competing refugee needs both abroad and in this country have made it more difficult for the U.S. to respond to the rising number of refugee applicants from the Soviet Union and around the world. Others question, especially in an era of *glasnost*, whether conditions are such for Soviet Jews that all emigrants from the USSR merit refugee status.

SOVIET JEWISH REFUGEES — BACKGROUND

Soviet Jewish emigration rates appear to be closely related to the condition of superpower relations. When tensions between the U.S. and the Soviet Union have decreased, emigration rates of Soviet Jews, along with those of ethnic Germans and Armenians, have increased. Conversely, when tensions were high, emigration rates declined. Today, increased rates of Soviet Jewish emigration also appear to be correlated with both the glasnost and *peristroika* policies and goals of Soviet leader Mikhail Gorbachev.

Until recently, those Soviet Jews allowed to emigrate from the USSR usually left with visas for Israel. Most traveled to Vienna and then Rome, where they sought resettlement, not in Israel, but elsewhere, usually in the United States. Those allowed to emigrate usually needed invitations from first-degree relatives (parents, children, spouses and siblings). Due to pressure from the West, the USSR allowed some, particularly those leaving with Israeli visas, to emigrate after receiving invitations from non-first-degree relatives. However, the Soviet government has denied, and continues to deny, permission to emigrate to some Soviet Jews because they are in possession of "state secrets." Others who have been denied permission were unable to obtain their relatives' formal approvals certifying that their departure will not cause economic hardship to those left behind.

RECENT EVENTS

At various times and in various forums, Soviet officials have hinted that they might change their emigration policies. These proposed changes have included: the repeal of the first-degree relative requirement; judicial review for familial consent; and a time limit for denying Soviet citizens permission to emigrate on the basis of access to classified information. In his December, 1988 speech before the United Nations, Soviet leader Gorbachev expressed much appreciation for the significance of the Universal Declaration of Human Rights which had been adopted approximately forty years earlier. He stated that a fitting way to observe the Declaration's anniversary was for a state "to improve its domestic conditions" for respecting and protecting the rights of its own citizens.

More recently, and to this end, the Supreme Soviet is considering legislation that would establish new laws on the exit from and entry into the Soviet Union. This legislation includes the following provisions:

— no invitation from relatives would be required for exit visas for short visits or for emigration purposes;

— every citizen automatically would receive passports, valid for five years, for foreign travel;

— every citizen would have the right to travel abroad for up to three years, with the possibility of extending the duration of stay through consular/diplomatic missions;

— all citizens would have the right to return to the USSR without conditions;

— the limit on state secrecy applications would not exceed five years, although this period may be extended in special cases; and

— refusal to issue an exit passport or denial of entry into the USSR may be appealed at any level of the process.

Such landmark legislation, although welcome, does not deal with some especially troubling issues. For example, the state secrets provision noted above would not prohibit the arbitrary extension of the five-year limitation. It also is unclear how this five-year limitation on state secrets would be applied to refuseniks who have been pressing to leave the Soviet Union for long periods of time. Furthermore, there are no provisions in the bill to deal with the poor relatives provision.

REACTION OF THE ADMINISTRATION TO INCREASED RATES OF SOVIET JEWISH EMIGRATION

The United States admitted a particularly large number of refugees from the Soviet Union in 1979 and 1980 (24,449 and 28,444 respectively). In subsequent years, refugee admissions from the Soviet Union decreased strikingly; for example, to 640 for all of 1985. Yet, regardless of this ebb and flow, the U.S. government's approval rate for Soviet Jewish refugees was high. However, as noted earlier, this situation changed with the increasing numbers of Soviet

Jews seeking entry into the U.S. as refugees. Refugee rejection rates increased and backlogs developed as people waited for interviews to determine their refugee status. At one point in mid-1989, about 15,000 people were waiting in Italy for their refugee adjudication, and in Moscow a large number of applicants were told that they might have to wait for as long as two years for their cases to be processed. (Backlogs in Moscow reached about 40,000 in late September, with more than 100,000 applications being distributed in Moscow as the October 1, change in policy, noted below, approached.) Additionally, processing at the U.S. Embassy in Moscow was halted twice in 1988, with the Embassy claiming that it had no budget or authority to grant greater than anticipated admissions. As an interim measure, Attorney General Thornburgh announced in December, 1988 that he had expanded his parole authority to admit to the U.S. those denied refugee status in Italy and up to 2,000 Soviet (largely Armenian) emigres per month from Moscow. More recently, the Attorney General directed Immigration and Naturalization Service (INS) officers in Italy to readjudicate all cases that had been denied refugee status. As a consequence, most Soviet Jews in Italy have been granted refugee status.

In other developments, the Administration announced that, as of October 1, all Soviets requesting refugee status will be interviewed in Moscow and all applications processed in the United States. Such a measure would essentially close down Italy as a route for Soviet Jews. The Administration also set another deadline that would further limit emigration to the U.S. Every prospective emigrant with properly dated Soviet exit documents would also have had to obtain Israeli visas by November 6, or forfeit the right to use the Vienna-Rome route to the United States. Consequently, those who obtained Israeli visas to leave the USSR by November 6, can journey to Rome, virtually the only path for Jewish emigration from the Soviet Union to the United States. Those unable to obtain an Israeli visa by November 6, must now apply directly to the U.S. for permission to emigrate. However, such permission will be difficult to obtain because of the regional ceiling on emigration from the Soviet Union — 50,000, of which 40,000, have been allocated for Soviet Jews. (The more than 30,000 Soviet Jews holding Soviet exit permits dated before October 1, and the 17,000 Soviets in the "pipeline," waiting in Rome and Vienna, will be given first priority. Since these numbers exceed the 40,000 refugee allocations for FY 1990, it is unlikely that any Jews in Moscow will be granted refugee status during this fiscal year.)

The Administration also helped develop legislation, H.R. 2646, introduced by Representative Lamar Smith (R-TX), that creates a new "special immigrant" category that would permit the entry, without government funding, of a limited number in special circumstances outside of the existing immigrant, refugee and parole categories. Such a measure, while offering needed flexibility, may in practice lead to circumstances in which people who merit refugee status would be instead granted this special immigrant status.

Much of the Administration's actions with regard to Soviet Jews have been based on the following assumptions:

— Soviet Jews should now undergo individual adjudication during which each must substantiate a well-founded fear of persecution;

— parole is a stopgap measure, to be replaced by special immigration legislation;

— privatization, *i.e.*, private sector initiatives, must become an even more central aspect of refugee resettlement; and

— interviews to determine refugee status should take place in Moscow, rather than in Italy.

REACTION OF THE CONGRESS TO INCREASED RATES OF SOVIET JEWISH EMIGRATION

With some notable exceptions and possibly disturbing trends resulting from the federal budget deficit, Congress has been very supportive of Soviet Jewish emigration and the granting of refugee status. In response to the current situation, many members of Congress have sent letters to the Departments of State and Justice, the INS, and Presidents Reagan and Bush protesting what they view as a shift in U.S. policy towards Soviet Jewish refugees.

Proposals introduced in Congress focus on funding to pay for resettlement, refugee status, and refugee numbers. H.R. 1605, the Emergency Refugee Act of 1989, was introduced by Representative Howard Berman (D-CA) to provide funds for overseas and domestic resettlement. (The FY 1989 supplemental appropriations bill included 75 million dollars to assist Soviet Jews, thereby covering much of that year's overseas funding.) Funds are now needed for FY 1990 overseas resettlement and the Voluntary Marching Grant domestic resettlement initiative. Legislation introduced by Senator Frank Lautenberg (D-NJ) and Representative Bruce Morrison (D-CT) deals with refugee denial rates. Their measure, signed into law on November 21, as an amendment to the Foreign Operations Appropriations bill, facilitates for FY 1990 the granting of refugee status to Soviet Jews and other groups. The legislation requires the Attorney General, in consultation with the Secretary of State and the Coordinator for Refugee Affairs, to establish categories of people from the Soviet Union, Vietnam, Laos and Cambodia "who share common characteristics that identify them as targets of persecution." The bill also requires the Attorney General to adjust to permanent resident status anyone from the Soviet Union, Vietnam, Laos or Cambodia who was granted parole into the United States between August 15, 1988 and September 30, 1989, after having been denied refugee status. Other members of Congress have taken different positions, with some asserting that Soviet emigres appear to qualify for, not refugee, but immigrant status. Some senators, including Alan Simpson (R-NY) and Strom Thurmond (R-SC), affirm that their goal is to ensure that "persons who are actually immigrants are not instead provided the benefits intended to meet the special needs of refugees." Clearly, the budget deficit has permeated much of the current debate in Congress, leading some to reformulate their opinion of who is or is not a refugee, the appropriate role of the federal government, and its partnership with voluntary agencies.

SELECTED ISSUES

Several issues have assumed increasing importance during the debate over the status of Soviet Jews. Clearly, the legal situation and budgetary crisis, discussed below, are noteworthy, with some suggesting that the entire situation is budget driven and that fiscal concerns have led to inappropriate interpretations of both law and custom. Of equal concern is the role, if any, Israel should play in the debate about the emigration and final destination of Soviet Jews. Another issue noted below is the pressure to accept a large number of refugees from other areas and, at the same time, offer assistance to those remaining in first-asylum countries. Also noted below is the relationship, if any, between Soviet emigration rates and glasnost and the impact of both on past and future trade agreement, one of which includes the Jackson-Vanik Amendment.

Legal Issues

Two related notions have been central to the granting of refugee status to Soviet Jews: that Soviet Jewish refugees have a "well-founded fear of persecution," and that, because of prevailing anti-Semitism in the USSR, Soviet Jews merit a "rebuttable presumption of persecution;" that is, unless proven to the contrary, Soviet Jews merit refugee status. Another related issue has to do with individual versus group determination. The 1980 Refugee Act authorizes annual refugee admissions to the United States of people "of special humanitarian concern" to this country. However, it was unclear at its passage whether the Act required the U.S., specifically the INS, to determine refugee status through individual, case-by-case, reviews or to continue presumptive eligibility for certain groups. Actions taken after the Act was passed, including a 1981 interpretation of the Refugee Act by the Justice Department's Office of Legal Counsel, a 1983 National Security Directive and an August 1983, INS *Worldwide Guidelines,* suggest that both individual and group determinations are compatible under the law.

Budget Issues

The U.S. faces expanding refugee assistance and resettlement needs with limited resources, largely the result of a federal budget deficit and Gramm-Rudman targets. Proposals to deal with the situation have included increasing both federal and private commitments, transferring unused funds from other immigration programs to refugee programs and converting much of the refugee program into a loan program. Soviet refugees are resettled in this country largely through the efforts of the Jewish community in general, which matches every federal dollar with two or three of its own dollars, and specifically through three voluntary agencies: the American Joint Distribution Committee (JDC), the Hebrew Immigrant Aid Society (HIAS), and the Council of Jewish Federations (CJF) and its local federations and affiliated agencies. Both public and private efforts will need additional federal funds for resettlement. Such shortage of funds practically mandates supplemental funding for the Soviet program during FY 1990. As noted by Senators Edward Kennedy (D-MA) and Paul Simon (D-IL) in a letter to Secretary of State James Baker.

> After years of promoting the exodus of Soviet Jews and others who have faced persecution in the past, the United States cannot now close the very door it has tried to open up for decades. Clearly, additional numbers must be forthcoming in this fiscal year — which, in turn, will probably mean additional funding. We cannot take funds for equally urgent refugee programs in other areas (which are already $58 million short), nor can we ask the private sector to fund more than 10,000 from the Soviet Union they are already expected to assist, given the severe strain the private voluntary organizations have faced over the past years (September 28, 1989).

The very realistic answer is supplemental funding for the Soviet program during the fiscal year.

The Controversy Over Destination

The controversy over the final destination of Soviet Jews, whether it be to the United States, Israel, or other countries, continues to this day. Clearly, ideological, political and financial concerns have emerged, in contrast to earlier years when a high percentage of Soviet Jews chose Israel as their final destination. In 1988, nearly 90 percent of exiting Soviet Jews resettled in countries other than Israel, most often in the United States. However, such statistics may shortly change, as Soviet Jews, realizing the roadblocks put up against emigration to the United States, decide to go instead to Israel. In November 1989 alone, about 18 percent, almost 2,500 Soviet Jews, decided to go to Israel. The Israeli government has strongly supported emigration to Israel, while opposing the granting of refugee status for those seeking U.S. entry. Many American Jews have been torn, wishing that Soviet Jews would settle in Israel, but also supporting freedom of choice. However, with the increasing numbers exiting the Soviet Union, many American Jews are supporting a two-track strategy of emigration to both the United States and Israel.

Equity Issues

The United States operates refugee resettlement and assistance programs which target groups throughout the world. Conservative estimates suggest that there are 15 million refugees worldwide, living in first asylum countries, along with another 15 million who are internally displaced within their countries. Especially because of the federal budget deficit, funds for resettlement and assistance often are viewed to be in competition. Furthermore, because the number of people from different parts of the world who wish to enter the United States as refugees always far exceeds the number allowed by law to enter, refugee policy must attempt to balance competing needs and priorities. At the same time, refugee policy should remain sufficiently flexible to respond to opportunities that result from both foreign policy successes and international disasters.

Refugee Status and Glasnost

Recent debate has focused on whether U.S. refugee policy toward Soviet citizens should be altered to reflect a changed Soviet environment under glasnost, in which a large number of Soviet citizens have exited, certain domestic freedoms have been granted, human rights safeguards have been proposed, prospects for East-West trade have improved and the country appears poised to pass landmark emigration legislation.

As welcome as these changes are, many view with alarm the increase in anti-Semitism and the rise in the number, strength and popularity of extreme Russian nationalist groups like *Pamvat*.

Soviet Emigration Rates and Trade Agreements

In the past, the United States has used trade as a leverage to negotiate with the Soviet Union. With relaxed emigration barriers and an increase in the number of Soviets, including Soviet Jews, being given permission to exit the Soviet Union, some have suggested that the Jackson-Vanik Amendment be temporarily waived. This amendment to the Trade Reform Act of 1974 instructs the President to refuse most-favored nation status (MFN) and U.S. government and investment guarantees to any "nonmarket" economy country that denies its citizens the right or opportunity to emigrate, imposes more than a nominal tax on emigration, or penalizes citizens as a consequence of their desire to emigrate. The President is authorized to waive these restrictions if he certifies to Congress that such a waiver would promote the objective of free emigration or that he has received assurances from the country receiving the waiver that its emigration policies will be liberalized. Those who support waivers argue that such initiatives, while economically insignificant, would send a positive and much-needed message to the Soviet Union. Others oppose a waiver until the new Soviet emigration law has been passed and implemented and related issues, including remaining refusenik cases, resolved. The American Jewish Committee supports the President's position as enunciated at the December, Malta Summit. When the President has received appropriate assurances with respect to the resolution of outstanding refusenik cases and the elimination of impediments to emigration such as the state secrets and poor relatives provisions, he has stated his support for extending a temporary waiver of Jackson-Vanik to the USSR. As noted earlier, these issues are addressed in the proposed emigration law now before the Supreme Soviet which probably will be approved this winter.

AMERICAN JEWISH COMMITTEE STATEMENT ON SOVIET JEWISH IMMIGRATION ISSUES

Taking the above events and issues into consideration, AJC adopted the following statement in November, 1989:

We are in the midst of one of the great migrations in Jewish history. Substantial numbers of Soviet Jews are leaving the USSR. For most of this century, Jews, as well as other Soviet minorities, were trapped in a country which persecuted them for their heritage and identity, but which prevented their flight to more receptive places. Under the glasnost and peristroika policies of the Gorbachev regime there has been change. Fifty to sixty thousand Soviet Jews will leave this year. Perhaps twice as many will leave next year, if exit permissions continue to be granted at the current rate. However, regardless of the number of emigres this year or next, there is still an urgent need to rescue as many Soviet Jews as expeditiously as is possible, and to assess and attend to the needs of Jews who, by choice or necessity, will remain in the USSR. At this time of profound change and opportunity for Jews in the Soviet Union, our long range goals for rescue must be reemphasized. These include:

— Exit as soon as is possible for the maximum number of Soviet Jews desiring to emigrate;

— An increase in the numbers of Soviet Jews seeking *aliyah* to Israel and improvement of Israel's capacity to receive them;

— A continued significant role for the United States in the rescue of Soviet Jewry, both through diplomatic means to assure their right to leave and through practical aid such as offering resettlement to refugees who choose to come here, especially for the purpose of family reunification;

— A smooth acculturation process for Soviet emigres who resettle in Israel or the U.S. and their absorption into the social, economic, cultural and private Jewish contexts of the country of their choice;

— Advocacy for other groups of refugees and maintenance of ethnic and religious coalitions for a generous refugee policy;

—A greater understanding of the social, political, economic and religious situation of Jews who remain within the Soviet Union and, development of practical programs to assist them;

— Close monitoring of anti-Semitism in its various political, nationalistic and cultural forms in the changing environment of the USSR.

— A special focus on those areas of Jewish population which rarely receive American and other Jewish visitors in order to facilitate emigration and reinforce aliyah for those who wish to go to Israel.

In order to achieve these goals, we need to have a solid grasp of conditions within the Soviet Union, the practical processes for securing exit and the actual reception capabilities of Israel and the United States, the major countries of refuge. We must be ready to adjust our strategy to work within ever changing conditions.

Procedures for exit and resettlement have recently changed in important ways. Current AJC policy and program, to be effective, must take account of these new developments, which include:

— Many more Jews are now able to leave the Soviet Union than ever before. The potential flow is likely to number in the hundreds of thousands. This represents a major victory for Jewish advocacy and American and Israeli diplomacy. But, at the same time, it puts a severe strain on American and Israeli capacities for absorbing this flow.

— Israel now sees an historic opportunity for attracting more Soviet refugees to the Jewish state. Greater exit means more potential immigrants to Israel. In addition, increasing numbers of Soviet Jews are visiting Israel. These tourists are providing the first eye-witness accounts of life in Israel. Yet, Israel faces a severe challenge of creating effective absorption programs and providing sufficient homes and jobs for the expected inflow. It has appealed to the United States for help, especially in the form of Agency for International Development housing loan guarantees. One point of contention has arisen over whether this new housing would be built on the West Bank, thus affecting the Israeli-Arab peace process. Israel has also called upon the world Jewish community to do more to improve the Israeli system of absorption.

— The United States has decided to accept as many as 40,000 Soviet Jewish refugees next year, a higher number than ever before. This represents a significant, though not the largest, proportion of total refugee acceptances of 125,000 for FY 1990. However, large as it is, this figure will still leave many Jewish refugees either waiting for long periods to get in or choosing to move to Israel. It also presents the need to develop a rational priority system to decide equitably who among refugee applicants should come to the United States. New plans have been offered in Congress to establish revolving loan funds or special immigration status that would allow more Soviet Jews to immigrate to the U.S., but provide less public funding for them. Passage of any of these plans would ease competition for entry but create new conflicts with Israel and impose a significant new financial obligation on American Jews.

— Refugee processing for entry to the United States has shifted in ways that will have a profound impact on prospects for Soviet Jewish entry. Previously, Jews left the Soviet Union with Israeli visas and applied for admission to the U.S. from Rome. As of October 1, processing has been shifted entirely to Moscow. This will end the misleading use of Israeli visas, but it will require many Jews seeking refuge to wait for long periods in the Soviet Union before they can move to America. A new political reversal could place them in grave danger. Moreover, American officials have been more likely to turn down applications for refugee status from applicants in Moscow than those in Rome. This is at least partly because private Jewish agencies such as HIAS have been able to advocate for potential refugees in Rome, while they have not been allowed to operate on Soviet soil. The shift in processing, which will save the American government and the Jewish community millions of dollars due to closing of facilities in Rome, carries with it the danger that more Jews will be denied refugee status by examining officials in Moscow.

— There is inadequate data on the Jewish identity and affiliation of Soviets who resettle in the United States. Knowledge about them is required to improve the outreach capacity to attract, welcome and integrate them into mainstream American Jewish life.

— Very little is known about Jews who live in the Soviet Union, both those seeking to get out and those who choose to stay permanently. It is vital to secure accurate information about the Soviet Jewish community so that programs adequate to its needs can be developed and implemented.

— It is also vital to track and analyze trends in anti-Semitism in the rapidly changing Soviet context.

This evolving fact picture requires decisive action by the American Jewish community. Over the coming months, we pledge our best efforts to:

— Secure the exit flow of Soviet Jews to the maximum degree possible.

— Promote aliyah to Israel, by working for U.S. government support and loan guarantees for housing consistent with U.S. guidelines for use of these funds and concerns for the peace process, by encouraging Israeli initiatives in housing, employment and education, and by playing a greater role in our private and organizational capacities to increase employment in Israel and to improve Israel's other acculturation capabilities.

— Monitor new U.S. refugee processing procedures to assure that they do not result in arbitrary and unjust denials of applications for refugee status for Soviet Jews and that they work effectively from the time of refugee application through movement to the country of resettlement. To achieve fairness in this new processing procedure, we support securing authorization for HIAS to open operations in Moscow. We also believe that we need to retain the option to reopen processing in Rome should Moscow operations prove unworkable or unjust. Intense scrutiny of processing by the U.S. Government and private groups is a key priority for the coming months.

— Develop clear guidelines for adoption by the U.S. government with respect to the process of decision making on refugee applications for Soviet Jews. Urge the effective implementation of legislation offered by Representative Bruce Morrison and Senator Frank Lautenberg and passed by Congress that would give a presumption of refugee status to this group.

— Maintain generous numbers for entry of Soviet Jewish refugees to the U.S. Next year's projected inflow of 40,000 will allow our country to continue to play a key role in rescuing Soviet Jewry. It is imperative now to secure both the public and private funds to assure that this resettlement is successful. One urgent priority is to secure government funding for the 10,000 refugee slots allocated to the Soviet Union for FY 1990 that are unfunded in the current budget. Any new unfunded

immigration status for Soviet Jews to allow those who can support
themselves to come in larger numbers must be carefully devised to
assure that it does not detract from opportunities for entry for those
who clearly merit refugee status and benefits.

— Continue to work for acceptance of other imperiled Jewish refugees
such as those from Iran and Syria, as well as refugee flows from
Indochina, Eastern Europe, Africa and Latin America who, like Soviet
Jews, have a well-founded fear of persecution.

— Maintain our ethnic and religious coalitions on behalf of Soviet
Jewish and other refugees and educate others about the continuing
Soviet Jewish need for exit.

— Continue to participate, as we have in the past few months, in
Immigration and Naturalization Service training programs for processing officials to apprise them of current challenges faced by Soviet Jews.

— Work with local communities to ease the acculturation of Soviet Jews
to their new surroundings and, in particular, to institutions and groups
that will strengthen their identification with the American Jewish
community. AJC can play a particular role in applying our findings on
acculturation to Soviet Jews, researching resettlement patterns and
successful programs, and compiling bibliographies of useful material.

— Provide accurate information to the U.S. and Jewish public on Soviet
Jews so needed efforts can be mobilized on their behalf.

— Conduct research in the Soviet Union on the current status and
needs of Jews there, as well as on the changing nature of anti-Semitism
in the USSR.

Carrying out this program will require prodigious effort and commitment
on the part of the American Jewish community and organizations such as
AJC. But at this historic moment of exodus and reception, we should do no
less.

13

Transforming Socialist Emigration: Lessons from Cuba and Vietnam

ROBERT L. BACH

State University of New York, Binghamton and
Carnegie Endowment for International Peace, Washington, DC

In the midst of every crisis there are seeds of a resolution. The problem is to identify those seeds and help them grow and blossom. Nine years ago, the United States was in the midst of its first asylum crisis following passage of the Refugee Act of 1980. That crisis, the Mariel boatlift, contained several dimensions that make it comparable to current experiences in Southeast Asia, especially the problems faced in Hong Kong as a result of the exodus from Vietnam. Comparisons between the migration experiences of Cuba and Vietnam have yet to be developed fully. Nevertheless, problems that emerged in each location highlight several features from which the international community and the United States should draw critical lessons.

The purpose of this paper is to examine briefly several dimensions of the current situation in Hong Kong in comparison with the historical experiences of Cuba. The paper also reports on research conducted during the last year in Hong Kong. The discussion is divided into several sections. The first draws attention to the similarities between Cuba and Vietnam. The second is a brief description of the research currently underway in Hong Kong. Section three turns to the character of rapid social change within Vietnam that complicates the understanding of the motivations for people leaving for Hong Kong. The fourth and final analytical section highlights several implications of this conceptual ambiguity for the screening process embarked upon by the Hong Kong government.

COMPARABLE EPISODES

The two most important similarities between the emigration flows from Cuba and Vietnam involve U.S. foreign policy and internal socialist reform. Whether Cuba in 1980 or Vietnam in 1989, the underlying problem was not the migration itself but its foreign policy implications. In both situations, responses to the uncontrolled character of the outflow were greatly complicated by the lack of formal diplomatic relations between the sending country and either the country of first asylum or the United States. Mechanisms for joint action and remedy were unavailable because they were impeded by U.S.-sponsored policies of economic embargo and diplomatic isolation. In each situation, the United States resisted changes in migration policy needed to respond effectively to the shifting nature of the outflow for fear that longer term foreign policy interests would be jeopardized.

The diversity of the social backgrounds of the people leaving Cuba and Vietnam also created similar political and practical problems for the country of first asylum. Historically, the international community and, especially, the United States have treated migrants from Cuba and Vietnam presumptively as refugees. Everyone who left was declared a refugee. The Mariel boatlift caused the United States to begin to question categorical eligibility for refugee status for Cubans. The primary reason was the obvious diversity among the origins of those arriving on U.S. shores."[1] Similarly, the shifting motivations and experiences of people leaving Vietnam today challenge the international community's search for a solution in Hong Kong and throughout the region.

The combination of these two features, foreign policy concerns and the complexity of refugees' social backgrounds, creates the primary practical problem facing countries of first asylum — controlling the flow in a way that the population may be screened effectively. In 1980, the United States lost for the first time its ability to screen people before they left Cuba. In Southeast Asia today, the flow of Vietnamese to Hong Kong offers no chance of prior screening. Who arrives in boats on Hong Kong shores is beyond the control of the host government.

In both situations, each receiving government faced the dilemma of accepting the burden of local resettlement or of returning people to a country which it believed was engaged in systematic practices of political persecution. The Mariel boatlift created serious problems of integration and permanent resettlement in the United States, especially in terms of providing aid to South Florida where most resettled. Detention camps provided for Cuban and Haitian immigrants also brought their inevitable problems. Although basic provisions were made available, conditions were substandard, riots broke out in several camps and prompted the use of military force to

subdue the population, and human rights were violated. The episode embar-
rassed the United States and resulted in one of the first times that charges of
human rights violations were levied by the international community against
the U.S. government's treatment of refugees.

Both governments also considered and, eventually, embarked on a plan
of repatriation. In 1980, the U.S. Government responded to the lack of control
over the boatlift by seriously considering, then rejecting, proposals to forcibly return some of the boat people to Cuba. One proposal planned to put
some of the exiles on boats, drive them to the U.S. naval base in Guantanamo,
and push them back on to Cuban territory. The proposal was rejected when
the U.S. Naval commander in Guantanamo requested formal instructions in
case the Cuban army pushed back.

Hong Kong faces a similar problem today because the Vietnamese government refuses to accept anyone returned against his or her will.[2] The U.S.
experience with its own first asylum crisis in 1980 provides valuable lessons
for this problem. Despite the antagonisms and drama of the events, the U.S.
and Cuban governments were able, given sufficient time, to work out an
agreement that allowed the United States to return to Cuba those whom it
considered undesirable and, under controlled circumstances, would have
screened out. This agreement, however, required the United States to recognize and announce publicly that people could be returned to Cuba without
fear of persecution or other mistreatment. In the same period, the U.S.
government also initiated its policy of interdiction of Haitian boats and their
forced return. Such a policy required the acceptance of the practice by the
Haitian government.

Few would have thought that in the midst of the U.S.-Cuban crisis that
both sides could come to a resolution that went far beyond the immediate
situation to establish a normal migration agreement. Few expect a similar
achievement in Hong Kong in the near future. Part of the disbelief is justified
because few could have anticipated the dramatic change in perspective that
occurred, in the case of Cuba, on both sides of the Florida straits that made
possible the transformation of the flow into a normalized situation. To the
Cubans, the radical change has involved accepting the view — somewhat
tentatively still — that people want to leave the country for "normal reasons,"
including primarily family reunification, and that not all or even most of the
emigrants have abandoned or by their actions have repudiated the Revolution. Recent interviews conducted in Havana with people who have applied
to leave, for instance, reveal that clear supporters of the Revolution are
among those who wish to leave to join family living permanently in Miami.[3]
In the United States, a normalized agreement also required a significant
change in position. As part of the normalized agreement, Elliot Abrams, then

Assistant Secretary for Latin American Affairs, had to certify that the United States could return people to Cuba without the expectation of fear of persecution. In addition, the U.S. accepted and expanded normal processing of applications for emigration in the U.S. Interests Section in Havana.

The process of achieving a normalized migration agreement such as the one obtained by Cuba and the United States interacts with a more significant change in the realities of people's lives in the country of origin. Even in the midst of the Mariel crisis, for instance, the characteristics and determinants of the outflow reflected systematic changes in socialist economic and political development and underdevelopment.[4] The systematic character of these changes creates problems for interpreting the reasons for people leaving the country of origin. In the following sections several of these problems and their implications have been highlighted.

DESCRIPTION OF RESEARCH PROJECT

In the Fall 1988, Myrna Candreia and the author initiated a research project on the flow of Vietnamese refugees to Hong Kong. Working with the Lutheran Immigration and Refugee Service and the United States Catholic Conference, the characteristics and conditions of the "long-stayer" population in the Hong Kong camps, the changing motivations for people leaving Vietnam, and the rapidly deteriorating possibilities for third country resettlement were examined.

The methodology for this part of the project involved three tasks. First, a sample of over 300 case files was drawn from the total population of persons interviewed by the U.S. voluntary agency personnel in Hong Kong. In this way, the reported experiences of Vietnamese who arrived throughout the 1980s, those who were accepted by U.S. Immigration and Naturalization Service (INS) interviewers as refugees, and those who have been denied refugee status were compared. Each case file contained detailed information recorded from several interviews conducted with the refugees, including the biographical, intake processing by the United Nations, the initial interview conducted by voluntary agency personnel, and notes taken by the INS interviewers. These files also contained information on the reason for the INS interviewer's decision and, frequently, supporting or dissenting reviews of these opinions by the refugee officer of the U.S. Department of State.

Second, statistical data on the biographical characteristics of all persons who arrived in Hong Kong over the last decade, whether they remained in the camps or had been resettled, were obtained. This statistical information includes demographic data and information on residential and occupational experiences in Vietnam both before and after 1975.[5]

Third, interviews with refugees in the Hong Kong camps and with voluntary agency personnel and U.S. government officials working in Hong Kong were conducted. The purpose of these interviews was not to obtain a statistically representative sample nor to attempt to establish a detailed account of reasons for fleeing Vietnam. But more systematic information was required than that obtained by others through impressions gathered during brief periods in the camps talking openly with only the refugees they encountered.

The purpose was more specific. The researchers' interviews to examine in more detail specific questions about items that had emerged from review of the case files were used. Interviews with refugees were approached with considerable caution, since interviews conducted by outsiders under camp conditions are a difficult enterprise and the reliability and validity of the information so obtained should be seriously questioned. The location of the interview and the status of the persons varied. Some had already received word that they had received refugee status and were shortly to be sent to the Philippines processing center for the eventual trip to the United States. These were interviewed in their native language in a nonthreatening atmosphere of the JVAR offices. Others were interviewed in the camps. That the interviews were voluntary and confidential was emphasized, — interviews were held in a separate, closed room — and interviewees' opportunities for acceptance for resettlement abroad were not in any way influenced. Refugees who fit broad categories of interests were selected, including whether they were from the North or the South, a man or a woman, and the year they arrived in Hong Kong.

Only material from the JVAR case files and from the interviews with refugees have been used. Except where specifically qualified, the evidence presented is from actual cases which represent a significant type of experience shared by many in the refugee population. Although the account of these experiences has obviously been rendered anonymous, these are real cases and have not been constructed as ideal typical cases to demonstrate a particular point.

TOWARD AN UNDERSTANDING OF SOCIALIST EMIGRATION

Research on refugees, especially those from socialist countries, has failed generally to draw upon well-established lessons acquired through studies of other forms of migration. Although differences among types of migration are often so compelling as to defy the need to make comparisons, theoretical insights from the general migration literature help to explain socialist emigration. For instance, in all forms, migration grows out of fundamental processes of social and economic change. Rather than abject poverty, economic collapse, or aberrant moments of persecution, migration usually responds to conditions of institutionalized and structured change, including growth, restructuring of the economy, and modernization.

The concept of "normal socialist emigration" relies on this central insight. Although persecution remains an important feature of flight, migration has increased during the last decade throughout the socialist world as a consequence of the pursuit of institutionalized growth and development. A combination of institutional changes that resulted from successful economic and social reform was even the cause of the drama and chaos of the Mariel crisis.[6] Similar institutionalized reforms are underway in Vietnam, and it is these changes that have given rise to the complexity of social backgrounds and motivations among those who flee their country for Hong Kong.

The interviews in Hong Kong captured one family's story that tells of this reform. The man had lived in Hai Phong, where until a year ago he was employed as a transportation worker for the State. As a transportation worker, he traveled throughout the Province and had contacts with many people and sectors. His wages were not good, he said, but his discomfort was moderated by the knowledge that the job was guaranteed. During this time, he had no plans or desires to leave his country. In the year before his departure, the State introduced economic reforms to Hai Phong in an attempt to stimulate economic enterprise. Private markets for buying and selling goods were allowed. The transportation worker said he perceived these markets as an opportunity for him to utilize the contacts he had made throughout the region to start his own business. He worked successfully as a marketeer for much of the first year, increasing his income over that received as a worker. At the end of the year, however, the State imposed a sixty percent tax on market activities in Hai Phong. Uncertain about his chances in the market with such a huge surcharge and angered by the intervention, he decided to leave the country in order to pursue his activities abroad.

Such an example is not representative of the majority of refugees interviewed in Hong Kong, or, for that matter, of those who have arrived from North Vietnam in the last few years. Still, it is a variation on an important theme. Liberalizing reforms and economic modernization are likely to create conditions in which people feel deprived and, for the first time, are able to seek alternative opportunities to overcome their repressive conditions. As they do, the origins of people leaving Vietnam — or as it has developed in Cuba — will diversify and challenge the perceptions of persecution that the international community has long held about these socialist countries. People will continue to leave Vietnam for reasons linked to persecution and out of experiences that are rooted in processes of socialist reform and economic modernization.

These internal social and economic reforms greatly complicate the process of determining whether people who leave their country by boat have a legitimate claim to resettlement opportunities by the international community. This difficulty is exacerbated by ideologically and politically-driven perspectives of potential resettlement countries. The international community has conducted very little research inside the country of origin or gathered reliable information about that country upon which to make decisions or even judgements about the motivations and experiences of people who leave.

The interviews with U.S. officials in Hong Kong, for example, revealed that INS interviewers often served as their own private researchers. Stacked next to their desks, the conscientious ones collect newspaper accounts and the rare article that passes their way that discusses changes inside Vietnam. The results are predictable. The information which provides INS interviewers a context for understanding individual refugee claims and, in some instances, is used in adjudicating an individual case, is selective, incomplete, and unintentionally biased. There is certainly no systematically organized body of information or analysis over which a critical international debate could emerge. Other than periodic updates on instances of political crimes in Vietnam from the U.S. Department of State, few other international groups have access to this critical stage in the international community's response to the Vietnam outflow. This is one reason the refugee determination process appears arbitrary to many observers.

From this research, several areas in which changes within Vietnam have complicated the interpretation of refugees' experiences and reasons for leaving have been identified. In each case, although various observers will insist on their own clear interpretation of these experiences, inconsistent, contradictory, and confused perspectives have been found. For present purposes, this discussion is limited to four areas, including compulsory labor, collectivization, former association and illegal departure.

Compulsory Labor

The case file reviews, interviews, and comparisons with Cuba have revealed that there is confusion about the meaning of compulsory labor in Vietnam and in socialist countries in general. In Hong Kong, U.S. interviewers often cite compulsory labor as the experience upon which they granted a person refugee status. Over the years, however, the interpretation of compulsory labor has varied from one interviewer to another. Compulsory labor in socialist Vietnam and Cuba consists of two forms of activities: obligatory or collective labor, and forced labor. Forced labor involves activities for which individuals or subgroups are singled out and is beyond what is normally performed by all. In the interviews and case file reviews, the best examples involve the selection of former members of the South Vietnamese army to perform especially hard, physical labor such as building ditches and repairing roads.

Collective, obligatory labor represents institutionalized, normal requirements of community life in socialist Vietnam and Cuba. However distasteful
for the highly individualized cultures of the United States, Canada and
others, socialized labor is expected of most citizens in Vietnam and Cuba.
Although the label "voluntary labor" is a misnomer, there are often only
foregone rewards rather than penalties that result from failure to fulfill the
requirement. A neighborhood block committee, for example, may require its
members to get up on a day of no work to spend the morning cleaning up
the community. Others may have to take turns at guard duty or other
community posts. This labor may also involve harder work, such as participating in the rice or sugar cane harvests, microbrigades for housing or
community building construction, and military reserve training.

We have observed a systematic pattern among U.S. INS interviewers of
confounding these two forms of socialist labor and of making contradictory
judgements about the significance of refugees' testimonies about compulsory
labor as the basis for refugee status. In some instances, one interviewer may
seek to determine the extent to which the labor performed could be considered out of the ordinary to the general community, while others used the
category of compulsory labor as a presumptive eligibility criterion.

Collectivization

A second area of interpretative confusion and differences involves the process of cooperativization in Vietnam, especially in cases involving refugees
from fishing villages. Most of the people leaving Vietnam for Hong Kong
come from the fishing areas of Hue, Da Nang, and Hai Phong. During the
process of collectivization of many of the fishing areas, the State has established incentives for fishers to leave their private boats and join the socialized
sector. People are invited to bring their privately owned boats into the
cooperative. They may refuse, and our interviews demonstrate that some do.
A consequence of refusing, however, is that the private fisher does not
benefit from the State's incentive plan. The State obviously supports fishing
cooperatives and has distributed access to fishing areas accordingly. Some
fishers who remain private benefit from their ownership of the boat and a
few have prospered. For many, however, remaining private results in economic hardship and inequality with those in the collectivized sector.

During the past few years, some INS interviewers have interpreted these
experiences as instances of political persecution. During our interviews in
Hong Kong, however, we discussed cases such as this one with other officials,
including a UNHCR legal advisor who laughed at the above example. "It is
typical U.S. thinking," the advisor said. "For those trained in a Western
European context, there is nothing unique or special about collectivization

— or about not participating in one." The variability in interpretation is clearly a problem and results largely from the lack of a sustained, open debate on differences of perspective.

Former Association

A third area of conceptual ambiguity involves the use of former association with the South Vietnamese government as a presumptive eligibility category for U.S. interviewers to grant refugee status. The original premise, justified by historical practice and commonsense, was that those who worked for or who had close relations with the U.S. government, members of the South Vietnamese government, and former soldiers of the defeated army would be subject to direct punishment upon the establishment of the new regime. Hundreds of thousands of such persons who were marched off to re-education camps and new economic zones provide solid support for such an assumption. In some cases, former associations are still very much the source of problems. The interviews and case file reviews repeatedly uncovered instances in which Vietnamese authorities had singled out people with a "bad background" — a phrase used by Vietnamese officials — to deny persons access to higher education or to send a household to a new economic zone.

History and especially generational change, however, have stretched the validity of these former associations and reduced their significance. In practice, the term former association now often refers to a second generation: those born in the early 1970s or after the regime change in 1975. Some of these younger adults report that they have family that was once associated with activities in the South before 1975. But the associations, as well as the family relations, vary from close to quite distant. The research sample, for instance, includes cases in which U.S. INS interviewers have granted refugee status to persons who indicated their relative had served in the South Vietnamese army even though the relative had died before they were born.

Within this context, there is also considerable variation within the sample in reports on the consequences that former associations now have in Vietnam. Some testify that they were mistreated because of their family's activities, while others, including some of those interviewed after they had already been granted refugee status, reported that even their father's ARVN service had not caused them any hardships. Part of this variation in experience is undoubtedly due to the uneven rule of law and central authority and local arbitrariness that characterizes Vietnam today. Still, traditional sources of persecution do not now appear to have consistent consequences among those who have fled Vietnam in recent years.

These variations, especially those linked to local authorities, support the existence of a pattern of "socialist discrimination." The term discrimination is specifically used to contrast it with persecution. Discrimination may be just as lethal and in terms of human rights as worthy of the international community's condemnation as persecution. But, to the extent that we recognize discrimination exists in all countries, it is no less significant within socialism. The basis of socialist discrimination may be different. It may result from a person's class background, or from an "ex- offender" experience, such as former association with the ARVN. It may also result from the consequences of having rewards distributed to those who actively participate in the Party's activities. Discovering and correctly interpreting the characteristics of differential social and economic treatment presents one of the more difficult tasks for those seeking to understand the motivations for leaving Vietnam and to improve the refugee determination process in Hong Kong.

Illegal Departure

Finally, a fourth area in which recent changes in Vietnam have created problems for existing interpretations of conditions and experiences that amounts to persecution is in official declarations concerning the concept of illegal departure. Reports from the Indochinese Refugee Action Committee (IRAC) and the Lawyer's Committee on Human Rights both correctly point out that Vietnam's Penal Code makes it a matter of national security and illegal for someone to leave the country without official authorization. Such constitutional provisions violate the United Nation's Declaration of Human Rights and its inclusion of the "right to exit" a country.[7] In Vietnam and Cuba, however, the exercise of this prohibition against leaving the country without authorization is much more complex and contradictory than indicated by the legal ban. According to Wayne Smith, who headed the U.S. Interests Section in Havana in 1980, one of the most important problems that led to the boatlift was the persistent, illegal seizure of boats by those who attempting to leave Cuba.[8] The Cuban government, which had signed an agreement with the United States against hijacking and piracy, expected the United States to return these "criminals" to Cuba for prosecution. Instead, the United States received them as refugees.

Several international observers have also commented on the contradictory demands placed on the Vietnamese government. On the one hand, the international community maintains that fundamental human rights include the right to leave a country and, in practice, that escape from persecution often requires a refugee to commit a crime in order to get away. On the other hand, in response to the large number of people who continue to leave Vietnam, the international community has pressured the Vietnamese government to control the outflow, including the use of police patrols along the coast to prevent people from leaving in boats.

These contradictory demands and pressures cannot be resolved while the motivations for leaving still prevail in Vietnam or Cuba. However, they re-emphasize the fundamental problem described at the outset of this discussion. Without formal, extensive diplomatic relations, and the political commitment to negotiate that characterizes these arrangements, responses to an uncontrolled outflow often create greater problems and intensify the abuses which lead to the emigration. Resolution lies in negotiating the conditions under which people can apply for exit and leave, because it is not illegal to leave, just illegal to leave illegally. Such an agreement is essentially the one negotiated between Cuba and the United States in 1984 and instated in 1987. The problems that arise from these difficulties result from the lack of participation of the socialist countries in the original discussions of the United Nation's Declaration of Human Rights. As more of these governments become willing to debate the issues, they should be brought into a broader, new international discussion on human rights principles for the 21st century.

While many of the categories used by U.S. INS interviewers to determine refugee status may have been stretched beyond their original empirical reference, others have been narrowed to the point that they do not reflect continued persecution in Vietnam. For example, the interviews and case file reviews have found that religious persecution remains a prevalent experience, especially in North Vietnam, and a reason for exit. Accounts of harassment of churchgoers by local officials was discovered. In one case, the refugee reported that local cadre confiscated his work permit the day before he attended church and arbitrarily returned it at varying periods afterwards. Without his work permit, he could not work on the state-owned fishing boat. This refugee and others also testified, however, that conditions had improved during the last decade. It was now at least possible to attend church services and the harassment is clearly a function of abuse by local authorities who, in many cases, are acting upon long-held, kinship-based feuds that have little to do with official policy or the goals of socialist reform.

In summary, historical changes within socialist countries have radically altered the empirical reference for many of the categories that the United States and the international community have used to determine refugee status. At the same time, the increasing diversity and complexity of these migrations have motivated many to expand further the definition of persecution and reasons for accepting people as refugees. In the United States alone, the concept of fear of persecution has been expanded by the Supreme Court's ruling on *Cardoso-Fonseca* to include a "reasonable fear of persecution." Perhaps more dramatically, the National Security Council has adopted a broader category of "expectation of admission" as grounds for accepting new groups of refugees.[9] As a result, there is little empirical clarity to the meaning of persecution and human rights that can be extended from location to location in the search for a consistent and fair determination of refugee status.

SCREENING

The conceptual and empirical confusion wrought by rapidly changing circumstances in socialist countries around the world have serious consequences for daily practices in the refugee determination process. For present purposes, three areas identified by the research in Hong Kong will be discussed. From this brief discussion, it is clear that screening procedures are not effective means — at least at present — for gaining control over migration flows and sorting out the confusion and political dilemmas that have resulted.

The Hong Kong government initiated screening with great fanfare on June 16, 1988, following the lead of other ASEAN countries, and quickly became the leading advocate of these practices in the international community. Screening, of course, is not new. As the Hong Kong government is quick to point out, the United States has been screening for years. The problem in this case is that Hong Kong is not screening; rather, it has implemented what is, in effect, a de facto immigration policy. It has instituted categories of admission and attached quotas to each category. That a screening process implemented to determine case-by-case claims to persecution produces the expected numbers in each category is perhaps the strongest indictment of the intentions of this new policy.

As Hong Kong announced implementation of its screening policy, it also predicted that 90 percent of those arriving by boat from Vietnam were normal, illegal economic migrants. Although the Hong Kong and British governments promised to adhere to the norms of asylum processing, this 90 percent would be eventually returned to Vietnam. Throughout the first year of screening, the rate of acceptance of refugees has fluctuated between 8 and 12 percent. This remarkable foresight among Hong Kong officials is, of course, a source of considerable concern among outside observers who are naturally suspicious of such predictive accuracy within a context of dramatic social change within Vietnam. Further examination of those "screened in," however, demonstrates the logic that lies behind the entire policy change.

The 10 percent of the cases which have been admitted to Hong Kong consist almost completely of those who arrived with family members already resident in the camps. This family reunion practice resulted from the insistence of the UNHCR at the time it was agreeing to serve as outside observer to the screening process. Only an extremely small number of cases have been accepted by the Hong Kong government as refugees on their merits.

Although the screening process has not been publicly discussed in this manner, the effect of these policy changes has established an immigration policy that closely matches the Hong Kong government's experiences with migration from the People's Republic of China. Most people who cross from the PRC into Hong Kong are treated as illegal economic migrants and, when apprehended, are quickly returned to the mainland. A much smaller fraction are admitted as normal family reunion immigrants. Only a very few who escape the PRC to claim political asylum in Hong Kong are accepted. These few are handled discretely by Hong Kong state security officials and quietly admitted so as not to embarrass and complicate political relations with the mainland. Responding to intense emotional and political charges that the Vietnamese were being treated better than family members from the PRC, the Hong Kong government has quietly, and under the guise of upholding international norms of first asylum, extended its immigration practice from China to Vietnam.

Second, the screening process suffers from the absence of an international debate on conditions within Vietnam and their implication for emigration. As pointed out earlier, immigration officials in Hong Kong are acting as essentially private researchers. The only primary source evidence they have is limited to the accumulation of testimonies from the refugees themselves. While these testimonies are valuable and necessary to the legal proceedings, by most rules of evidence they are inadequate. This is especially true in a context in which changes in the overall conditions at home may be altering the meaning and empirical reference of established forms of behavior and experiences. Refugee testimonies may be both honest and accurate, but by their nature they do not capture the full range of experiences in the country of origin that would promote a better understanding of the changing conditions.

Third, in the absence of sustained debate and rigorous analysis, the rules of evidence used in the screening process become paramount to influencing the decision. As the Lawyer's Committee on Human Rights has argued effectively, the extension of a benefit of the doubt to persons seeking asylum in Hong Kong is fundamental. Several cases in which different officials reviewed the same applications have been examined. There is undoubtedly a dramatic shift in the decision when the interviewer gives the benefit of the doubt to the applicant. If the validity of refugees' testimonies are fundamentally challenged, it is possible to deny large groups of arrivals. As a result, when and under which circumstances officials give refugees this benefit becomes a primary source of variation in the outcomes of the determination process.

CONCLUSION

During a period of such rapid change, history is still writing the conclusions to this analysis. If lessons can be drawn from previous episodes of similar crises, however, the dimensions of a resolution lie primarily in two areas: the foreign policies of states within Southeast Asia and, especially, of the United States, and the course of socialist reforms within Vietnam. The options for responding practically to the refugees are well defined and familiar to the practice of international law and the work of the UNHCR. The central questions depend on the political choices currently under negotiation.

This analysis points to several dimensions of the problem that should influence the political choices. First, the absence of formal, diplomatic relations as a part of the problem, both in terms of failing to respond to the uncontrolled outflow and in exacerbating conditions inside Vietnam that cause the exodus. Second, the goal of political resolutions to this crisis should be to normalize the emigration flow, placing the process squarely within the established practices of states' migration policies within the region. Orderly departure programs, although a step in the right direction, do not provide the support for the eventual depoliticization of the emigration, but rather, institutionalize the political tensions.

Finally, the value of refugee policy as an instrument of U.S. containment strategies is diminishing globally as changes in the socialist world render this historical basis of foreign policy outdated.[10] Although U.S. relations with Cuba and Vietnam are different than with Eastern Europe, changes in U.S. global strategy should undoubtedly alter attitudes and practices toward emigration from these two traditional sources of refugees. The time for reassessment of U.S. policy toward both Vietnam and Cuba is long overdue. The present opportunity to make positive changes in migration policies would constitute a valuable first step.

FOOTNOTES

[1] For a discussion, See Bach et al., "The Flotilla Entrants: Latest and Most Controversial," Cuban Studies (11), 1981.

[2] At the time of redrafting this paper, the Hong Kong government has forcibly returned 51 persons to Vietnam. There are also signs of a negotiated compromise to this dilemma, allowing ordering return to Vietnam in exchange for guarantees of safe treatment.

[3] These interviews were conducted in 1989 as part of a Ford Foundation-sponsored research exchange between myself and a group of researchers at El Centro de Estudios Sobre America, Havana. The interviews were conducted by Rafael Hernandez and Redi Gomis.

[4] See Robert L. Bach, "Emigration and Socialist Construction: Lessons from Mariel," Cuban Studies (15), 1985.

[5] Some of the results from the statistical analyses have been presented publicly in Robert L. Bach, "The Hong Kong Refugee Dilemma," presentation at the Carnegie Endowment for International Peace, December 20, 1989, and in Robert L. Bach and Myrna Candreia,"Vietnamese Refugees in Hong Kong." Institute for Research on Multiculturalism and International Labor, forthcoming, January, 1990.

[6] Of course, within the last year, large-scale migration has been produced by reforms throughout the Soviet Union and Eastern Europe. While much of this emigration simply results

from release of pent-up political opposition and repressed groups, I would argue that the forces of economic reform — *perestroika* — have also unleashed incentives to emigrate throughout the Soviet bloc. A cautionary, analytical note is also warranted. Reforms in Eastern Europe and the Soviet Union, and their obvious effects on emigration, are not likely to be easily repeated in Cuba or Vietnam. While the economic and political fates of both countries are tied to Eastern Europe and the Soviet Union, the extent of internal opposition, possibilities for significant economic reform, and the degree of direct Soviet control make Cuba and Vietnam unlikely candidates in the short term for the type of political reforms that have captured the world's attention. *See*, Robert L. Bach, "Perestroika in Cuba?", unpublished paper, Institute for Research on Multiculturalism and International Labor, State University of New York, Binghamton, 1989.

[7] *See* Alan Dowty, *Closed Borders: The Contemporary Assault on Freedom of Movement*. New Haven: Yale University Press, 1987.

[8] *See* Wayne Smith, *Closest of Enemies. A Personal and Diplomatic Account of U.S.-Cuba Relations Since 1957*. New York: W.W. Norton and Co., 1987.

[9] "Expectation of admission" was used by the National Security Council and the U.S. Department of Justice to justify the use of parole in the case of the greatly expanded number of Soviets allowed to leave their country. While there is no question that U.S. foreign policy has created such an expectation among, in particular, Soviet Jews, the concept is so imprecise — and the use of support for emigration as a tool of U.S. foreign policy so pervasive — that it accurately describes refugee and family reunification situations around the world.

[10] *See* Paul H. Kreisberg, "Containment's Last Gasp," *Foreign Policy* (75), 1989.

14

Voluntary Repatriation

JOHN MCCALLIN
Representative, UNHCR

Voluntary Repatriation as a durable solution to refugee problems is of intrinsic interest and an area of activity of increasing importance and significance. It is, furthermore, often a controversial activity, and one where the role of UNHCR is often misunderstood.

The Office of the High Commissioner for Refugees was established in 1950, and the Statute outlining the scope of the Office's activities identified voluntary repatriation as one of the principal solutions to the refugee problem. The High Commissioner should *inter alia* seek permanent solutions to the problem of refugees by assisting governments to facilitate voluntary repatriation. Similar sentiments were expressed in the General Assembly resolution adopting the Statute and the General Assembly has repeatedly stressed voluntary repatriation as a solution. Specific attention has been paid to this subject by the Executive Committee of the High Commissioner program and will be addressed in this article.

In the early years UNHCR's role was confined essentially to facilitating voluntary repatriation through the provision of travel papers and means of transport. Interest in the returnee essentially ended at the border with his homeland.

Today, however, the UNHCR is more active in promoting voluntary repatriation and it is increasingly recognized internationally that the High Commissioner has a legitimate interest in the fate of returnees and that his involvement need not and should not terminate at the border but should continue until the returnee is safely reintegrated. UNHCR involvement in this context means two things essentially: first, monitoring that returnees are not harassed or penalized in contradiction to any amnesties or guarantees for their safety provided by their country of origin; secondly, depending on the conditions, helping to sustain and consolidate the return of that person through the provision of economic assistance.

For UNHCR, voluntary repatriation — stressing the word voluntary — is the best solution in terms of both protection, and durable long term solutions. By so stating we mean that the returnee stands to regain economic, social and political rights; to reacquire land and property, etc. Indeed more may be acquired if the process leading to the return has resulted in the removal or amelioration of the problem that first forced exile.

This is clearly so when, as in the case of Zimbabwe's independence, a new political order develops. This is certainly the hope for Namibia and for Afghanistan. But the gain can also be seen, for example, in the repatriation of Ethiopians from Djibouti. Here the mechanism which helped to create the conditions favorable to return was through the establishment of a tripartite commission which enabled the concerned governments and UNHCR to examine what needed to be done to enable people to return. Principal elements in the agreement provided for the voluntary character of the return and assurances by the Government that returnees would be exempt "from all prosecutions for any crime committed by him for political purpose before he left Ethiopia."

UNHCR was to be allowed access to returnees both to see that returnees were not mistreated, and to see to the provision of assistance to them necessary to secure their reintegration and self sufficiency.

Here, the real evolution and the real gain is in the increasing recognition internationally that UNHCR has a right to promote repatriation and to monitor in the country of origin the welfare of those who have repatriated. Tripartite agreements such as that between Ethiopia, Djibouti and UNHCR have now become the norm whenever a repatriation is contemplated. How has this come about?

Over time, as experience with voluntary repatriation has deepened and in ongoing consultations with governments, voluntary agencies and UNHCR's own management body — the Executive Committee — this experience has been evaluated and the good lessons learned. Experience with voluntary repatriation programs is embedded within forty years of more general experience with a broad range of refugee needs both of a protection and assistance nature. Our mandate is to protect refugees but also to find durable solutions to their problems which are in their best interest. UNHCR was created to deal with the problem of refugee but we are as equally conscious that refugees have "problems," and this must influence and color the search for solutions.

There are situations, and some would say the majority, where because of resource limitations, or the massive nature of the influx, or because of national legislation, or for a variety of reasons, refugees in a country of asylum face a bleak and uncertain future. Not necessarily legally — their protection may be assured in the sense that they can remain in their country of asylum — but economically and culturally as well, the context of their exile may simply preclude their decent and adequate self-sufficiency, may deny an adequate education to their children, or access to land and employment. Moreover, very few refugees relinquish the desire to return one day to their homeland.

An appreciation of the quality of exile, or the lack of it, turns the spot light upon the durable solutions available; i.e., local integration, resettlement in third countries, or voluntary repatriation. There are between 12 and 14 million refugees worldwide at this time — resettlement for a significant number of them is not a likely prospect for achieving local integration and in many situations is not promising.

At the same time international attention is being directed more at the causes of refugee flows; with a dual objective of first trying to head off future disruptions that might force people to cross international borders and secondly, to bring about conditions conducive to voluntary repatriation.

This discussion is increasingly seen not just within the context of Refugee law, but within the wider framework of Human Rights law; particularly the right of people to leave and return to their country and the obligation of governments to create for their citizens conditions wherein they can live their lives in peace and prosperity.

The way this type of concept is evolving can be seen clearly in two conclusions on repatriation adopted by UNHCR's Executive Committee.[1]

The first conclusion reached in 1980 was relatively brief. It stressed that repatriation should be voluntary and that, given appropriate conditions, it was the best solution for refugee problems. At the freely expressed wishes of refugees to return home, the governments of the country of origin and asylum should take the necessary steps to facilitate repatriation. It was suggested that refugee representatives should be enabled to return home, see for themselves how conditions are, and report back to their compatriots. Formal guarantees of safety to returnees should be issued and scrupulously respected. As regards the role of UNHCR, it was stated that UNHCR should be "appropriately" involved.

Five years later, in 1985, this subject was revisited by the Executive committee. In a much larger and more detailed discussion the Executive Committee covered much new ground and discussed root causes:

> The aspect of causes is critical to the issue of solution and international efforts should also be directed to the removal of the causes of refugee movements. Further attention should be given to the causes and prevention of such movements, including the coordination of efforts

currently being pursued by the international community and in particular within the United Nations. An essential condition for the prevention of refugee flows is sufficient political will by the States directly concerned to address the causes which are at the origin of refugee movements (Conclusion on the International Protection of Refugees, UNHCR, No. 40 (XXXVI), (c), p. 86).

The next paragraph dealt with the responsibilities of States:

The responsibilities of States towards their nationals and the obligations of other States to promote voluntary repatriation must be upheld by the international community. International action in favor of voluntary repatriation, whether at the universal or regional level, should receive the full support and cooperation of all States directly concerned. Promotion of voluntary repatriation as a solution to refugee problems similarly requires the political will of States directly concerned to create conditions conducive to this solution. This is the primary responsibility of States (Conclusion on the International Protection of Refugees, UNHCR, No. 40 (XXXVI), (d), p. 86).

An active role was recommended for the UNHCR. As opposed to the 1980 language on an "appropriate" role, now it is recommended that the High Commissioner act as a channel of communication between all parties with a view to promoting repatriation. "On all occasions" — not just as appropriate — the High Commissioner should be fully involved in the feasibility, planning and implementation of repatriation.

Perhaps most significantly it is stated in the conclusion:

The High Commissioner should be recognized as having a legitimate concern for the consequences of return, particularly where such return has been brought about as a result of an amnesty or other form of guarantee. The High Commissioner must be regarded as entitled to insist on his legitimate concern over the outcome of any return that he has assisted. Within the framework of close consultations with the State concerned, he should be given direct and unhindered access to returnees so that he is in a position to monitor the amnesties, guarantees or assurances on the basis of which the refugees have returned. This should be considered as inherent in his mandate. (Conclusion on the International Protection of Refugees, UNHCR, No. 40 (XXXVI), (1), p. 88).

Now conclusions of the Executive Committee are in no way legally biding upon states, but they are useful pointers to the way in which matters are proceeding and help to orientate governmental thinking about important issues. Parties to the discussion include those who give and those who receive refugees as well as those who finance solutions to their problems; thus, all points of view are represented, with UNHCR representing the refugee, but all parties share that responsibility.

The impression should not be given that UNHCR favors or is the mouth-piece for those who see voluntary repatriation as an expedient rather than the best solution. UNHCR's approach is rooted firmly in the individual's right to return to his home and if he expresses the wish to do so then UNHCR stands ready to facilitate repatriation in all its phases from negotiation with the governments concerned to the logistical details of the physical return.

Monitoring repatriation thus, has moved from the situation in earlier days when UNHCR simply facilitated movements to the point now where the organization is able to promote voluntary repatriation, suggest guarantees for returnees, follow up on their welfare and to assist them to reintegrate through the provision of assistance. By fostering discussion internationally about the root causes of refugees flows, UNHCR is implicitly seeking the means to prevent them, and in this regard is enlisting the wider cooperation of the UN and the international community to orient their thinking and their action to this end.

FOOTNOTE

[1] Full text of both conclusions is reproduced in the appendix to this article.

APPENDIX

Conclusions on the
International Protection of Refugees

adopted by
the Executive Committee of the
UNHCR Programme

Published by the
OFFICE OF THE UNITED NATIONS
HIGH COMMISSIONER FOR REFUGEES — UNHCR

1980 (Executive Committee — 31st Session)

No. 18 (XXXI) VOLUNTARY REPATRIATION *

The Executive Committee

(a) *Recognized* that voluntary repatriation constitutes generally, and in particular when a country accedes to independence, the most appropriate solution for refugee problems;

(b) *Stressed* that the essentially voluntary character of repatriation should always be respected

(c) *Recognized* the desirability of appropriate arrangements to establish the voluntary character of repatriation, both as regards the repatriation of individual refugees and in the case of large-scale repatriation movements, and for UNHCR, whenever necessary, to be associated with such arrangements;

(d) *Considered* that when refugees express the wish to repatriate, both the government of their country of origin and the government of their country of asylum should, within the framework of their national legislation and, whenever necessary, in co-operation with UNHCR take all requisite steps to assist them to do so;

(e) *Recognized* the importance of refugees being provided with the necessary information regarding conditions in their country of origin in order to facilitate their decision to repatriate; recognized further that visits by individual refugees or refugee representatives to their country of origin to inform themselves of the situation there — without such visits automatically involving loss of refugee status — could also be of assistance in this regard;

---

* CONCLUSION ENDORSED BY THE EXECUTIVE COMMITTEE OF THE HIGH COMMISSIONER'S PROGRAMME UPON THE RECOMMENDATION OF THE SUB-COMMITTEE OF THE WHOLE ON INTERNATIONAL PROTECTION OF REFUGEES.

(f) *Called* upon governments of countries of origin to provide formal guarantees for the safety of returning refugees and stressed the importance of such guarantees being fully respected and of returning refugees not being penalized for having left their country of origin for reasons giving rise to refugee situations;

(g) *Recommended* that arrangements be adopted in countries of asylum for ensuring that the terms of guarantees provided by countries of origin and relevant information regarding conditions prevailing there are duly communicated to refugees, that such arrangements could be facilitated by the authorities of countries of asylum and that UNHCR should as appropriate be associated with such arrangements;

(h) *Considered* that UNHCR could appropriately be called upon — with the agreement of the parties concerned — to monitor the situation of returning refugees with particular regard to any guarantees provided by the governments of countries of origin;

(i) *Called* upon the governments concerned to provide repatriating refugees with the necessary travel documents, visas, entry permits and transportation facilities and, if refugees have lost their nationality, to arrange for such nationality to be restored in accordance with national legislation;

(j) *Recognized* that it may be necessary in certain situations to make appropriate arrangements in co-operation with UNHCR for the reception of returning refugees and/or to establish projects for their reintegration in their country of origin.

No. 40 (XXXVI) VOLUNTARY REPATRIATION *

The Executive Committee,

Reaffirming the significance of its 1980 conclusion on voluntary repatriation as reflecting basic principles of international law and practice, adopted the following further conclusions on this matter:

(a)   The basic rights of persons to return voluntarily to the country of origin is reaffirmed and it is urged that international co-operation be aimed at achieving this solution and should be further developed;

(b)   The repatriation of refugees should only take place at their freely expressed wish; the voluntary and individual character of repatriation of refugees and the need for it to be carried out under conditions of absolute safety, preferably to the place of residence of the refugee in his country of origin, should always be respected;

(c)   The aspect of causes is critical to the issue of solution and international efforts should also be directed to the removal of the causes of refugee movements. Further attention should be given to the causes and prevention of such movements, including the co-ordination of efforts currently being pursued by the international community and in particular within the United Nations. An essential condition for the prevention of refugee flows is sufficient political will by the States directly concerned to address the causes which are at the origin of refugee movements;

---

* CONCLUSION ENDORSED BY THE EXECUTIVE COMMITTEE OF THE HIGH COMMISSIONER'S PROGRAMME UPON THE RECOMMENDATION OF THE SUB-COMMITTEE OF THE WHOLE ON INTERNATIONAL PROTECTION OF REFUGEES.

(d)   The responsibilities of States towards their nationals and the obligations of other States to promote voluntary repatriation must be upheld by the international community. International action in favour of voluntary repatriation, whether at the universal or regional level, should receive the full support and co-operation of all States directly concerned. Promotion of voluntary repatriation as a solution to refugee problems similarly requires the political will of States directly concerned to create conditions conducive to this solution. This is the primary responsibility of States;

(e)   The existing mandate of the High Commissioner is sufficient to allow him to promote voluntary repatriation by taking initiatives to this end, promoting dialogue between all the main parties, facilitating communication. It is important that he establishes, whenever possible, contact with all the main parties and acquaints himself with their points of view. From the outset of a refugee situation, the High Commissioner should at all times keep the possibility of voluntary repatriation for all or for part of a group under active review and the High Commissioner, whenever he deems that the prevailing circumstances are appropriate, should actively pursue the promotion of this solution;

(f)   The humanitarian concerns of the High Commissioner should be recognized and respected by all parties and he should receive full support in his efforts to carry out his humanitarian mandate in providing international protection to refugees and in seeking a solution to refugee problems;

(g)   On all occasions the High Commissioner should be fully involved from the outset in assessing the feasibility and, thereafter, in both the planning and implementation stages of repatriation;

(h)   The importance of spontaneous return to the country of origin is recognized and it is considered that action to promote organized voluntary repatriation should not create obstacles to the spontaneous return of refugees. Interested States should make all efforts, including the provision of assistance in the country of origin, to encourage this movement whenever it is deemed to be in the interests of the refugees concerned;

(i) When, in the opinion of the High Commissioner, a serious problem exists in the promotion of voluntary repatriation of a particular refugee group, he may consider for that particular problem the establishment of an informal *ad hoc* consultative group which would be appointed by him in consultation with the Chairman and the other members of the Bureau of his Executive Committee. Such a group may, if necessary, include States which are not members of the Executive Committee and should in principle include the countries directly concerned. The High Commissioner may also consider invoking the assistance of other competent United Nations organs;

(j) The practice of establishing tripartite commissions is well adapted to facilitate voluntary repatriation. The tripartite commission, UNHCR, could concern itself with both the joint planning and the implementation of a repatriation programme. It is also an effective means of securing consultations between the main parties concerned on any problems that might subsequently arise;

(k) International action to promote voluntary repatriation requires consideration of the situation within the country of origin as well as within the receiving country. Assistance for the reintegration of returnees provided by the international community in the country of origin is recognized as an important factor in promoting repatriation. To this end, UNHCR and other United Nations agencies as appropriate, should have funds readily available to assist returnees in the various stages of their integration and rehabilitation in their country of origin;

(l) The High Commissioner should be recognized as having a legitimate concern for the consequences of return, particularly where such return has been brought about as a result of an amnesty or other form of guarantee. The High Commissioner must be regarded as entitled to insist on his legitimate concern over the outcome of any return that he has assisted. Within the framework of close consultations with the State concerned, he should be given direct and unhindered access to returnees so that he is in a position to monitor fulfillment of the amnesties, guarantees or assurances on the basis of which the refugees have returned. This should be considered as inherent in his mandate;

(m) Consideration should be given to the further elaboration of an instrument reflecting all existing principles and guidelines relating to voluntary repatriation for acceptance by the international community as a whole.

15

The Case for a Mandatory and Enforceable Safe Haven Policy in the United States

ARTHUR C. HELTON

Director
Refugee Project of the Lawyers Committee for Human Rights

According to the Immigration and Naturalization Service, at least four million undocumented persons currently reside in the United States.[1] Many have come because of instable conditions or war in their home countries. In this regard, a formal safe haven program in the United States is needed. Pending legislation is in this vein, including special legislation to give protection to Chinese, and the Moakley-DeConcini bills which would delay the deportation of Salvadorans and Nicaraguans. A comprehensive mechanism must be established to decide in what instances to provide protection for categories of undocumented persons who should not be forced back to face civil war or general unsafety in their home countries through apprehension and deportation, or the inability to subsist without authorization to work under immigration employment controls.

There has been much debate over the past several years[2] about the need for a new safe haven policy in the United States for the protection of individuals who do not qualify under law as refugees.[3] Traditionally, such protection has been accorded through grants of "extended voluntary departure" by the Attorney General and Secretary of State. Over the past 29 years, thirteen different nationality groups have been given this administrative status which protects against forced removal.[4] But commentators, including many in the nongovernmental community, have expressed concern about the lack of enforceable criteria and standards for granting humanitarian protection to nonrefugees. Foreign affairs and immigration enforcement priorities have seemed to dominate decisionmaking in this area, generally to the exclusion of humanitarian considerations.[5]

The need for a new safe haven policy has also been sharpened by employment controls which were introduced as an immigration reform measure in 1986. Employers are prohibited on pain of sanction from hiring those persons (including aliens) who cannot furnish appropriate documentation showing that they are authorized to work.[6] Undocumented persons who before may have been able to secure effective haven as a result of inconsistent agency enforcement and bureaucratic inefficiency now have difficulties in subsisting as a result of the new employment controls.

As a consequence of both concern with the apparently political character of decisionmaking under the current system and the 1986 employment controls, many in the nongovernmental community began discussing an alternative. The proposal under discussion has two basic points: 1) the Attorney General would be required to grant Safe Haven to nationals of foreign states experiencing "armed conflict," and; 2) determinations made by the Attorney General with respect to the existence of armed conflict in a foreign state would be subject to review by the judicial branch.

The term "armed conflict" in the proposal is founded in the language and negotiating history of the Geneva Convention Relative to the Protection of Civilian Persons in Time of War, August 12, 1949, (entered into force October 21, 1950, hereinafter referred to as the "Geneva Convention") and the Protocol Additional to the Geneva Conventions of 1949, (Protocol II) June 8, 1977, (hereinafter referred to as the "Protocol").[7] Unlike these instruments, however, the proposed definition of "armed conflict" would combine what the Geneva Convention and the Protocol define separately as "international" and "non-international" armed conflict into one single concept of "armed conflict." This concept is based upon the existence of armed conflict between two states as defined in Common Article 2 of the Geneva Convention, or armed conflict between forces acting under the authority of a state and armed dissident forces as defined under Article 1 of the Protocol. Persons fleeing situations of armed conflict face the same types of threats to their personal safety whether those conflicts are of an "international" or "non-international" character. Therefore, the distinction is abandoned for these purposes.

The concept of "non-international armed conflict" first appeared, without definition, in Common Article 3 of the Geneva Convention:

> In the case of armed conflict not of an international character occurring in the territory of one of the High Contracting Parties, each party to conflict shall be found to apply, as a minimum, the following provisions.

The Commentary on Common Article 3 reveals that the Diplomatic Conference debate about this issue centers around the development of objective criteria for determining what constitutes a non-international armed conflict. Specifically, the Commentary refers to the intent of the drafters in Common Article 3 to include "civil wars" within the scope of the Convention. Several criteria aimed at defining these terms were proposed and rejected by the Conference, including: involvement of the armed forces of a government against an organized military opposition; control of part of the national territory by the opposition group, and designation of a civil war by the United Nations. In the end, however, the Conference could not agree on a common formulation of "non-international conflict" and chose not to define the term.

Not until recently has some measure of international consensus been reached on the definition of non-international armed conflict. Article 1 of the Protocol Additional to the Geneva Convention provides the following formulation of non- international armed conflict. This definition forms the basis of the "armed conflict" concept in this proposal:

> This Protocol, which develops and supplements Article 3 Common to the Geneva Conventions of 12 August 1949 without modifying its existing conditions of application, shall apply to all armed conflicts which are not covered by Article 1 of [Protocol I] and which take place in the territory of a High Contracting Party between its armed forces and dissident armed forces or other organized armed groups which, under responsible command, exercise such control over a part of its territory as to enable them to carry out sustained and concerted military operations and to implement this Protocol.
>
> This Protocol shall not apply to situations of internal disturbances and tensions, such as riots, isolated and sporadic acts of violence and other acts of similar nature, as not being armed conflicts.

The Diplomatic Conference clarified the concept of non-international armed conflict by selecting a number of material elements which would be considered sufficient evidence of the existence of an armed conflict. For the purposes of defining "armed conflict" in the safe haven context, the formulation similarly limits the discretion of those making decisions concerning whether or not a situation qualified as an armed conflict.

Under this proposal, the Attorney General is provided with objective criteria on which to base determinations about safe haven determinations.[8] Once the elements of armed conflict are satisfied, the Attorney General would be required to grant safe haven to persons from these affected regions already in this country. These decisions would be subject to judicial review.

Traditionally, haven has been accorded as a matter of administrative discretion. This general power should be retained. However, a central purpose underlying this new nongovernmental proposal is to provide objective criteria for determining when safe haven must be granted. Past proposed safe haven legislation has employed the concept of "ongoing armed conflict" as one of the standards for determining whether to invoke a safe haven designation.[9] These proposals, furthermore, have expressly exempted from judicial review the Attorney General's determinations under the statute.[10]

The proposed "armed conflict" concept still provides the Attorney General with discretion in interpreting the particular factual circumstances underlying the conflict according to international standards. This discretion, however, is not intended to be absolute and is reviewable by the federal courts under this proposal. Specific criteria which a court can use to review the Attorney General's determination are provided. Thus, under the terms of the Administrative Procedure Act, a court can ensure that the decision is not "arbitrary, capricious, an abuse of discretion or otherwise not in accordance with law."[11]

Nor would such review be barred by the political question doctrine.[12] This doctrine is required to make a policy determination clearly unsuitable for judicial consideration or where the issues cannot be resolved through judicially manageable standards. Judicial review of the Attorney General's determinations under the armed conflict criteria would not present unreviewable political questions outside the scope of judicial competence.

Although determinations as to whether or not an ongoing armed conflict exists in a particular country may have foreign policy implications, that fact alone would not bar judicial review. As the Supreme Court has stated, "it is error to suppose that every case or controversy which touches foreign relations lies beyond judicial competence."[13] Determinations as to whether a foreign conflict rises to the level of an "armed conflict" do not turn on policy issues such as foreign relations or immigration concerns;[14] in fact, those considerations should be entirely absent from the analysis. Rather, the armed conflict determination is to be based on the ascertainment of factual circumstances such as whether the armed forces possess the necessary organization and control of territory as to enable them to carry out "sustained and concerted military operations." These are issues of fact which the judiciary can competently evaluate.[15]

Many technical details remain to be worked out in this proposal, including the exact mechanism by which members of the public can request a designation from the Attorney General, the appropriate venue for judicial review, etc. Also, other issues must be addressed, and provision should be made for social benefits for recipients of safe haven. Past bills have sought to prohibit benefits.[16] But this prohibition has been one of political expediency bereft of any humanitarian consideration. Additionally, those who have remained in the United States for several years should have an opportunity to become permanent residents. Current immigration provisions recognize that a durable status may be warranted for persons who have developed substantial ties to the United States.[17] There is no reason beyond expediency not to extend a similar benefit to those who have been accorded safe haven.

FOOTNOTES

[1] *NY Times*, June 18, 1989, at A.24.

[2] *See* U.S. Catholic Conference, *Toward New U.S. Statutory Standards for Those Who Flee Crises: Humanitarian and Political Responses* (1988); Lawyers Committee for Human Rights, *A Preliminary Discussion of Considerations in Enacting Temporary Refuge Legislation* (1987); Refugee Policy Group, *Safe Haven: Policy Responses to Refugee Like Situations* (1987). Congress in 1981 passed a resolution urging that the Reagan Administration consider civil strife in El Salvador in relation to extended voluntary departure. Pub. L. No. 97-113, §731.

[3] Under U.S. statute, refugee protection in the form of admission or asylum is reserved for those who have a "well-founded fear of persecution" because of "race, religion, nationality, membership in a particular social group or political opinion." 8 U.S.C. §1101(a)(42)(A).

[4] Lawyers Committee for Human Rights, *supra* note 1, at appendix 1. The Attorney General's recent program of one-year deferred departure for Chinese nationals present in the United States as of June 5, 1989, could be considered a specie of extended voluntary departure.

[5] *See* note 2 *supra*.

[6] 8 U.S.C. §1324. *See* Helton, "A Gap in the Immigration Law," *Wash. Post*, Aug. 19, 1987, at A23.

[7] Perluss and Hartman, "Temporary Refuge: Emergence of a Customary Norm" 26 *Virginia J. of Intl. L.* 551, 602-12 (1986).

[8] Perluss and Hartman, *supra note 7*, at 605 n.246.

[9] *See, e.g.*, H.R. 1355, 101st Cong., 1st Sess., at §2(b).

[10] *Id.* at §2(h).

[11] *See* 5 U.S.C. §702(2)(A).

[12] *See Hotel & Restaurant Employees Union* v. *Smith*, 594 F.Supp. 502 (D.D.C. 1984).

[13] *Baker* v. *Carr*, 369 U.S. 186, 211 (1962).

[14] *See Quinn* v. *Robinson*, 783 F.2d 776, 788 (9th Cir. 1986) ("we fail to see why a judicial acknowledgment that terrorist groups exist would constitute a 'recognition' of those groups in the sense of legitimizing their actions"); *Tel Orren* v. *Libyan Arab Republic*, 726 F.2d 774 (D.C. Cir. 1984) (noting that that judicial acknowledgment of the effect of the Palestine Liberation Organization on the foreign relations of the United States does not grant that group any form of "official recognition").

[15] *See Eain* v. *Wilkes*, 641 F.2d 504 (7th Cir. 1981) (court not barred by political question doctrine from construing application of treaty's political offense exception involving determination of whether there exists violent political turmoil at the site and time of individual's alleged illegal activities); *Quinn* v. *Robinson*, 783 F.2d 776 (9th Cir. 1986) (same). *See* also Helton, "Harmonizing Political Asylum and International Extradition; Avoiding Analytical Cacophony," 1 *Georgetown Imm. L.J.* 457 (1986).

[16] *See, e.g.*, H.R. 45, 101st Cong., 1st Sess., at §303; H.R. 1355, 101st Cong., 1st Sess., at §2(e).

[17] *See* 8 U.S.C. §§1254(a) and 1255a.

16

Asylum Claims from a Judicial Perspective

WILLIAM R. ROBIE
Chief Immigration Judge
U.S. Department of Justice

ASYLUM

Statutory Authority

I. & N. Act §208(a) provides that: "The Attorney General shall establish a procedure for an alien physically present in the United States or at a land border or point of entry, irrespective of such alien's status to apply for asylum, and the alien may be granted asylum in the discretion of the Attorney General if the Attorney General determines that such alien is a refugee within the meaning of section 101(a)(42)(A)."

Establishment of "prima facie" eligibility for asylum

In order to prevail in a claim for asylum, an alien must establish 1) that he or she has a well-founded fear of persecution; 2) that such persecution is based on the alien's race, religion, nationality, membership in a particular social group, or political opinion; and 3) that asylum should be granted in the exercise of discretion. I. & N. §101(a)(42)(A).

The standard for a well-founded fear of persecution

In *Cardoza-Fonseca* v. *INS*, 107 S. Ct. 1207 (1987), the Supreme Court held that a well-founded fear of persecution is a reasonable fear, not to the level of a clear probability of persecution.

The Board of Immigration Appeals (BIA), in *Matter of Mogharrabi*, Int. Dec. 3028 (1987), adopted the reasonable fear test; that an alien possesses a well-founded fear of persecution if a reasonable person, in his or her circumstances, would fear persecution if he or she were returned to their native country.

To establish a reasonable fear, the BIA has held that an alien must show: 1) that he or she possesses a belief or characteristic that a persecutor seeks to overcome by means of punishment; 2) that the persecutor is aware, or could become aware, that the alien possesses this belief or characteristic; 3) that the persecutor has the means, or capability, to punish the alien; and 4) that the persecutor has the inclination to punish the alien. *Matter of Acosta*, Int. Dec. 2986 (1985); *Matter of Mogharrabi.*

Fear is both objective and subjective

1) The subjective criteria for fear is met if the alien is indeed fearful. *Matter of Acosta; Guevara-Flores* v. *INS*, 786

F.2d 1242 (5th Cir. 1986). 2) The objective criteria for fear is met if the fear has a basis in reality, or is a reasonable probability. *Matter of Acosta; INS* v. *Stevic*, 104 S. Ct. 2489 (1984).

Persecution

1) Persecution is defined as a showing that harm or suffering will be inflicted upon the alien as a punishment for possessing a belief or characteristic that the persecution seeks to overcome. *Guevara Flores* v. *INS*. 2) Persecution usually must be inflicted by the official government, unless the government refuses, or is unable, to protect the individual against persecution instigated by other groups. *Matter of McMullen*, 17 I. & N. Dec. 542 (1980).

Burden of proof and countervailing equities

A person can have a well-founded fear of persecution even when the probability of persecution is less than 50 percent. *Cardoza-Fonseca* v. *INS*.

Since it is obviously difficult for an alien fleeing persecution to obtain corroborating evidence, an alien's own credible testimony, supported by general documentary evidence of conditions in the country of persecution may suffice. *Bolanos-Hernandez* v. *INS*, 767 F.2d 1277 (9th Cir. 1984).

1) While any determination of the credibility of the applicant by the Immigration Judge must be supported by the record, an Immigration Judge's determination is given great weight by the BIA. *Matter of Bromand*, 17 I. & N. Dec. 450 (1980). 2) The BIA stated in *Matter of Mogharrabi*, that since an alien's own testimony may be the only evidence available, it will suffice, in the Immigration Judge's discretion, when it is believable, consistent, and sufficiently detailed to provide a plausible and coherent explanation of the basis for the asylum application. *See* also K. McGrath, "Credibility Determinations:

Avoiding Adverse Findings in Asylum Hearings and Defeating Them on Appeal," 16 *Immigration Newsletter* 3 (1987). 3) If no finding of credibility is made, at least one circuit has presumed the alien's testimony to be credible. *Artiga* v. *INS*, 829 F.2d 720 (9th Cir. 1987); *Canjura-Flores* v. *INS*, 784 F.2d 885 (9th Cir. 1985).

An alien's circumvention of orderly refugee procedures, in and of itself, is generally not sufficient to warrant a discretionary denial of asylum. *Matter of Pula*, Int. Dec. 3033 (1987).

While it has been long-settled that it is not persecution for a country to require military service of its citizens, asylum eligibility could arise if: 1) the country's penalty for refusal to serve was disproportionately severe, and the refusal to serve was based on a protected characteristic; or 2) if the alien would be required to engage in inhuman conduct as a result of the required military service. *Matter of A — G —*, Int. Dec. 3040 (1987).

An alien need not prove a claimed persecutor's exact motive for his or her persecution. *Matter of Fuentes*, Int. Dec. 3065 (1988).

Coerced recruitment into an army or guerilla forces does not establish persecution on the basis of race, religion, nationality, membership in a particular social group, or political opinion. *Matter of Maldonado-Cruz*, Int. Dec. 3041 (1988).

State department advisory opinion

Before the Immigration Judge can render a decision on the asylum application, the application must be forwarded to the Bureau of Human Rights and Humanitarian Affairs (BHRHA) in the Department of State. There are three possible responses: 1) BHRHA may have no opinion and will refer the Immigration Judge to the State Department's *Country Reports on Human Rights Practices*. 2) BHRHA may have a general opinion which applies to all applicants from that nation, region, or particular group; or 3) BHRHA may provide a specific opinion relating to the alien question.

The BHRHA opinion is only advisory in nature, is provided to both parties and becomes a part of the hearing record.

WITHHOLDING OF DEPORTATION

Statutory authority

I. & N. Act §243(h)(1) provides that: "The Attorney General shall not deport or return an alien (other than an alien described in §241(a)(19) (Nazi war criminals) to a country if the Attorney General determines that such alien's life or freedom would be threatened in such country on account of race, religion, nationality, membership in a particular social group, or political opinion."

Standard of proof

The alien must demonstrate a clear probability of persecution, and the alien bears the burden of proof. *Matter of Acosta; INS* v. *Stevic.*

If the alien meets this burden, withholding of deportation is mandatory. *INS* v. *Stevic.*

The standard of proof is higher (a "clear probability of persecution" versus a "well-founded fear of persecution,") in withholding of deportation. *Cardoza-Fonseca* v. *INS.*

But the alien must still demonstrate a fear of persecution (*Matter of Acosta*), similar, but stronger, to that under §208(a).

STATUTORY BARS TO ASYLUM AND WITHHOLDING OF DEPORTATION

Persecution of others

An alien is ineligible for asylum and withholding of deportation if he or she has ordered, incited, or assisted in the persecution of others on account of race, nationality, religion, membership in a particular social group, or political opinion. I. & N. Act §101(a)(42)(B).

Danger to national security

An alien may be denied asylum or withholding of deportation if he or she poses a danger to the security of the United States. I. & N. Act §243(h)(2)(D).

Criminal convictions in the United States

An alien may not be granted asylum or receive a withholding of deportation if the alien has committed a particularly serious crime, constituting a danger to the community of the United States. I. & N. Act §243(h)(2)(B). Note the implications that may follow from the provision that an alien is conclusively presumed to be deportable if he or she has committed an "aggravated felony." Anti-Drug Abuse Act of 1988 §7347(a), Pub. L. No. 100-590 (November 18, 1988), 102 Stat. 4181.

The IJ will consider the nature of the conviction, the underlying circumstances relating to the crime, the type of sentence imposed, and whether the alien will be a danger to the community. *Matter of Frentescu*, 18 I. & N. Dec. 244 (1982); *Crespo-Gomez* v. *Richard*, 780 F.2d 932 (11th Cir. 1986).

Criminal convictions outside the United States

An alien is ineligible for relief if he or she has committed a serious non-political crime outside the United States. I. & N. Act §243(h)(2)(C).

It is a non-political crime if the act was committed without a genuine political motive. Even if the alien's motivation was political, the crime may be considered a serious non-political crime if the act is disproportionate to the political objective, or if the act can be deemed atrocious or barbarous (*e.g.* an act of terrorism). *McMullen* v. *INS*, 788 F.2d 591 (9th Cir. 1986).

PRACTICAL CONSIDERATIONS OF AN IMMIGRATION JUDGE IN AN ASYLUM HEARING

Credibility

Is the alien's testimony supportive of the application for asylum and consistent with its contents? Does the alien's demeanor, allowing for cultural differences and communication difficulties, enhance the believability of the alien's testimony?

Evidence

Is the evidence submitted relevant to the country and the alien? Is the evidence organized, explained, and submitted in a logical and non-cumulative manner?

Country conditions

Does the country genuinely persecute groups for their beliefs and actions, or is it experiencing economic and social turmoil, or, if both, which applies more to the alien seeking asylum? Is the alien a member of any group experiencing persecution? Are his or her concerns unique or are they spread throughout the entire country?

Preparation of asylum application

Is the application completed in a manner that fully explains the alien's claim, or will the Immigration Judge be forced to flesh-out the facts? Does the application contain stock answers that have little or no bearing on the individual in question? Is the alien eligible for a grant of asylum? For a period of time, a number of Immigration Judges accelerated cases by pretermitting applications from aliens that were statutorily ineligible for asylum. The BIA ended this practice in *Matter of Gonzalez*, Int. Dec. 3071 (1988).

Other considerations

If the alien committed a crime in his or her country and is not statutorily barred from being granted asylum, how serious was the criminal act? How old was the alien at the time? What is the penalty for that crime in the country to which the alien would be deported? How strong are the alien's views that are involved in the alleged persecution? What will happen to him or her if he or she is deported?

PART V
IRCA'S EMPLOYER SANCTIONS PROVISIONS

17

Enforcing IRCA's Ban on Employment Discrimination

LAWRENCE J. SISKIND

Special Counsel, Office of Special Counsel for Immigration Related Unfair Employment Practices

The Office of Special Counsel (OSC) was created by the Immigration Reform Control Act of 1986 (IRCA) to enforce IRCA's ban on employment discrimination. Section 102 of IRCA prohibits employment discrimination based on national origin and citizenship status. It covers discrimination in hiring, firing, and recruitment or referral for a fee. Section 102 reflects Congress' concern that sanctions against employers for hiring unauthorized workers would result in this type of discrimination.

ACCOMPLISHMENTS OVER THE PAST YEAR

The past year has been an extremely active one for the OSC, both in enforcing section 102 and in making the law more workable. IRCA's antidiscrimination provision followed much debate and compromise in Congress. The resulting provision was, in many ways, complicated and unwieldy. Working within the language of the statute to make it simpler for victims of discrimination to enforce their rights, OSC has made adjustments in four areas.

First some sense was put into the procedures aliens must follow to show that they are intending citizens who may assert citizenship status discrimination claims. Form I-772, the Declaration of Intending Citizen, was created to enable authorized aliens to show their intent to become citizens, something they must do to qualify for citizenship status protection. Confusion arose, however, in regard to the filing requirement. This was not specifically addressed in the statute or the regulations implementing section 102. The preamble to the regulations stated that the form had to be filed before the alleged discrimination. But the instructions on the form stated that filing it was only a prerequisite "to assert a claim," not to qualify for protection.

To compound the problem, the form wasn't widely available to authorized aliens who could qualify as intending citizens. Few people knew about the form, let alone the filing requirement.

To dispel the confusion, on March 24, 1988, a notice was published in the *Federal Register* that made it clear that it was not necessary to file the I-772 before the alleged discrimination. The filing requirement was satisfied as long as the form was completed and filed before the discrimination charge was filed with the Office of Special Counsel. This has since been codified in a regulation issued by the Attorney General.

The filing requirement was made more workable by changing where the form has to be filed. The I-772 is an INS form. Originally, it could only be filed with the INS. But since the form's only purpose is to meet the statutory requirement to file a citizenship status discrimination charge, many aliens logically, though incorrectly, assumed that it should be filed with the Office of Special Counsel. Misfiled forms delayed processing of charges. The OSC brought this problem to the attention of the INS, and an agreement was made to appoint the Special Counsel as agent for receiving I-772s. Under this agreement, announced in the *Federal Register* October 17, 1988, I-772s can be filed either with the INS or the OSC.

A second change was also related to the "intending citizen" requirement. Among the classes of aliens who can be intending citizens, are temporary residents under IRCA's legalization program. But it was unclear whether temporary resident status began from the time of application for legalization or once the status was actually granted. This question became crucial for enforcement of section 102. Many months pass from the time individuals apply for legalization to the time when their applications are approved. In some cases, the process takes years. The Office of Special Counsel found that it was consistent with the language of the statute, the legislative history of section 102 and the comparable INS procedures, to protect successful applicants while their applications were pending.

The Attorney General was urged by OSC to issue a regulation announcing that successful legalization applicants are protected from citizenship status discrimination from the time they apply for legalization.

A third area of adjustment has been in the statute's division of jurisdiction. The Equal Employment Opportunity Commission (EEOC) and the Office of Special Counsel both have jurisdiction over employment discrimination based on national origin. But the OSC's jurisdiction only extends to employers with four to fourteen employees. The EEOC has jurisdiction over employers with fifteen or more employees. Also, the prohibition on citizenship status discrimination, which is only enforced by the OSC, covers all employers with four or more employees.

Congress was careful to make sure that the OSC and the EEOC did not have overlapping jurisdiction. But actual discrimination claims do not always fall neatly or exclusively within the jurisdiction of one office. The OSC often receives charges alleging both national origin and citizenship status discrimination against employers with fifteen or more employees. And even when it is clear to lawyers where the charge should be filed, it is not always clear to laypersons — who are usually the people who file charges. There was concern that the delay caused by misfiled charges would cause individuals to lose their rights due to filing deadlines.

For this reason, the OSC and the EEOC entered into an interim Memorandum of Understanding appointing each agency the agent of the other for the purpose of receiving charges under Title VII and section 102. A timely charge filed with the wrong agency stops the clock for purposes of the filing deadline. In other words, a deserving party will not lose precious time just because the form was filed with the wrong office.

This interim Memorandum of Understanding will soon be made final. The final version will also include provisions for referring charges between the agencies and coordinating investigations of related charges.

The OSC has invited 114 state and local civil rights enforcement agencies to enter into similar agreements. In September an agreement was signed with the Human Rights Division of the New Mexico Department of Labor. Agreements are being developed with: the Florida Commission of Human Relations, the Kansas Commission on Civil Rights, the Louisville and Jefferson County Human Relations Commission, the Michigan Department on Civil Rights, the Minnesota Commission on Human Rights, the Montana Human Rights Commission, the New Hampshire Commission for Human Rights, the New Haven Commission on Equal Opportunity, the City of New York Commission on Human Rights, the Pennsylvania Human Relations Commission, the Rhode Island Commission for Human Rights, the South Carolina Human Affairs Commission, the Tennessee Human Rights Commission, and the Wyoming Fair Employment Commission.

Finally, the OSC made protection under section 102 more comprehensive by including an antiretaliation provision in the regulations. The provision protects individuals who have filed a charge, intend to file a charge, or who have otherwise participated in a section 102 investigation or proceeding, from retaliation by the their employer. In the past year, two complaints alleging retaliation were filed. In one case, the employer settled almost immediately. The other case resulted in a trial; decision in that case is pending.

ENFORCEMENT OF SECTION 102

As of March 1989, the OSC had received 490 charges of discrimination. Of these, 300 are closed. Twenty-six were dismissed without investigation because of lack of information. Of the remaining 274 closed cases, the OSC settled 62 cases, usually for back pay and reinstatement — close to 25 percent. A case over which the OSC had jurisdiction and where reasonable cause was found has never been closed without first obtaining full relief for the victim of discrimination.

The impact of the work or the OSC has gone beyond the individual charges filed. Entire industries have reformed their employment policies due to the OSC's efforts. This is particularly true of the airline and defense industries.

Far-reaching settlements were negotiated with Pan Am, American Airlines, United Airlines and Northwest Airlines. Pan Am, United, and American had refused to hire flight attendants who were not U.S. citizens or permanent residents with green cards, and Northwest required pilots to be U.S. citizens. After settlement with the OSC, each of these airlines will now hire U.S. citizens and intending citizens (temporary residents, permanent residents, asylees, and refugees) for these positions.

Defense contractors have also changed their policies. Northrop Corporation, McDonnell Douglas, Ford Aerospace, and Lockheed all had hiring practices which excluded one or more classes of aliens who are intending citizens. As a result of intervention, they will now employ all classes of intending citizens.

Additional advances have been accomplished with other federal agencies to bring their regulations into compliance with IRCA. For example, during the investigation of a charge against Northrop Corporation, the OSC discovered State and Commerce Department regulations which Northrop and other defense contractors had construed as restricting employment to U.S. citizens and permanent residents. The OSC worked with state and commerce officials and persuaded them to clarify their policies so that contractors could hire all classes of intending citizens. The commerce department's new policy has since been codified in its regulations.

These changes in the airline and defense industries have opened tens of thousands of jobs previously closed to authorized alien workers.

CHALLENGES AHEAD

Education has always been a priority with the OSC. In actuality most employers do not want to discriminate, and will not, once they understand the law. But as pointed out by the General Accounting Office (GAO) in its second annual report on the implementation of employer sanctions, too many employers remain unaware of their antidiscrimination responsibilities.

The challenge is to launch an extensive education campaign in a time of severe budget restraints. Despite the Office's lack of a sufficient number of staff members, continuous efforts are made to meet the program's goals.

An outreach task force, similar to that recommended by the GAO in its second annual report, is the best hope for meeting this challenge. The GAO recommended that the Attorney General direct the Special Counsel to set up a task force of federal agencies, including the INS, the EEOC, and the Department of Labor (DOL). The task force would develop a coordinated strategy for educating the public about IRCA's antidiscrimination provision. Even before the GAO recommendation, the Office of Special Counsel had been working closely with the INS, the EEOC, and the DOL on coordinating outreach. The OCS will continue to need the help of these agencies, particularly the INS, for a really effective outreach campaign, and is committed to working with the INS toward this end.

CONCLUSION

Over the past year, the OSC received ten times as many charges as the previous year — but only four new lawyers have been added to the staff. It can be confidently predicted, however, that in the coming year the anti-discrimination provision will be enforced the same way it was this past year — competently and vigorously — because of the dedication of the staff of the Office of Special Counsel to meet the challenge.

18

Report on the Implementation of Employer Sanctions

ARNOLD P. JONES
Senior Associate Director, General Accounting Office[1]

The results of the General Accounting Office's (GAO) second annual report to Congress on the implementation of employer sanctions and the work GAO plans to do for the third and final report will be discussed in this presentation.

Background information on GAO's mandate will be presented. The Immigration Reform and Control Act (IRCA) requires GAO to issue three annual reports to Congress and each of these reports is to answer the following three questions: have employer sanctions 1) been implemented satisfactorily, 2) caused a pattern of discrimination and 3) resulted in an unnecessary regulatory burden for employers? Congress did not define the key terms in these questions — specifically, "implemented satisfactorily," "pattern of discrimination," or "unnecessary burden." As a result, GAO will have to interpret Congress' intent. When the final report is issued later this year, it will include the results of the General Counsel's research of the legislative history for these key terms.

SECOND REPORT FINDINGS

"Satisfactory" Implementation

How were these three questions answered in the second and most recent report to Congress? On the first question, it was concluded that the Immigration and Naturalization Service (INS) had implemented employer sanctions satisfactorily but could improve its efforts to measure employer compliance with the law. Specifically, GAO supported INS' overall approach of continuing to educate employers while increasing enforcement actions.

On the basis of GAO's November 1987 employer survey, about 22 percent of the nation's employers were not aware the law existed and as many as 20 percent of those aware of the law did not clearly understand the law's major provisions. Furthermore, about 50 percent of the employers surveyed had not completed the required I-9 forms for their new employees. Clearly, there was a need for more education on the law.

INS' enforcement actions were satisfactory. As of September 1, 1988, 452 employers had been cited for knowingly employing unauthorized aliens and 4,700 had been cited for not completing I-9s. Before being cited, each employer was educated on the law's requirements and given the opportunity to voluntarily comply. Few employers had appealed their fines and none of those that did appeal prevailed before the judge. These are indications of a program that is being implemented satisfactorily.

As mentioned earlier, Congress had not defined what is meant by "satisfactorily implemented." GAO has interpreted "satisfactory" to mean a report card grade of "C" or better, since Congress did not ask the GAO to determine if the law's implementation had been "perfect" or "without fault." Recommendations were made to the attorney general that, if carried out, could raise INS' grade to an "A."

The first recommendation was for INS to begin systematically collecting data on aliens' use of fraudulent or counterfeit documents to complete the I-9 form. Based on the review of INS' records in five cities, it was found that about 40 percent of the aliens apprehended at work had used "bad paper" to get their jobs. However, these data were not readily available and were not routinely being reported to Washington. Congress intended for the I-9 form to be a barrier against unauthorized alien employment and INS and Congress need to know how frequently that barrier fails.

The second recommendation was for INS to begin measuring employers' compliance with the law differently. INS gave employers several chances to comply but only measured and reported compliance at the end of the process. Specifically, INS sends employers a letter notifying them that their I-9 records are to be inspected in about a week. Then INS visits the employer and, if not in compliance, will educate them on the proper way to complete the forms. Then INS will return at another time. It is not surprising that INS reports over 90 percent of employers are brought into compliance through these enforcement actions.

This process gives every employer the chance to comply before being fined. However, INS should begin reporting the compliance rate it finds at the beginning of the process, because INS can probably visit no more than one percent of the nation's employers every year. Only 50 percent of the employers in the GAO's survey were in compliance — a lot lower than INS is reporting. If this law is to succeed, the 99 percent of the employers that INS does not visit are going to have to voluntarily accept the need to complete I-9s. INS can begin to measure this voluntary compliance rate by recording what percent of employers were in compliance when first receiving INS' notice of inspection. INS and Congress need this information to accurately assess the law's effects.

The third recommendation was related to improving the INS and Department of Labor's (DOL) quality controls for inspecting I-9 forms. GAO accompanied INS and DOL on a visit to 100 employers and found that frequently the inspectors did not verify that I-9 forms had been prepared for all new employees. For example, the agent would often walk in to the employer's office, ask to see the I-9 forms, and not look at the employer's payroll records to assure all required forms had been completed. It would be more effective if an agent were to quickly review the payroll, looking for the names of persons hired after the law was passed but who have not completed I-9s. Unless this or similar checks, are done routinely, the government may never find out that the employer hired unauthorized aliens or did not complete the forms for other employees. Both INS and DOL have concurred with GAO's recommendations and are currently taking implementation actions.

Patterns of "Discrimination"

Have employer sanctions resulted in a pattern of discrimination against authorized workers? There are three elements to this question: 1) caused by the law, 2) pattern and 3) against authorized workers. These three elements are very important to the interpretation of the results of GAO's employer survey.

The number of discrimination complaints filed with the Office of Special Counsel (OSC) and EEOC were relatively low: 286 and 148 respectively as of September 1988. However, many people who are discriminated against will not — for various reasons — file a formal complaint with a government agency. For this reason, GAO looked for another method to measure discrimination. Six thousand employers, randomly selected from a list of over 6 million employers, were anonymously surveyed. Various questions that would measure potential discriminatory hiring practices were asked. It was determined that when projecting the results to the universe of employers surveyed, about 16 percent, or 528,000 employers who were aware of the law, had begun unfair employment practices. Specifically, these employers were only asking "foreign-looking" or "foreign-sounding" persons to present documents or began a policy to hire only U.S. citizens.

GAO concluded that this was not a pattern of discrimination because two of the three critical elements mentioned earlier were not present. First, it could not be concluded from the survey how many authorized workers were not hired as a result of these practices. It may be that employers, after seeing the documents presented by the "foreign-looking" people, went ahead and hired them. In addition, those "foreign-looking" people who were not able to present documents may have been unauthorized aliens and were not supposed to be hired. The second element not present from the survey results was "caused by the law." Employers who had the unfair employment practices were asked if they began the practice because of the employer sanctions provision. While the majority did, the numbers were too low to statistically project. With these two elements missing, GAO was unable to conclude that the law has caused a pattern of discrimination against authorized workers. However, policymakers should be concerned about employers who may have begun unfair employment practices. GAO recommended that the attorney general direct the OSC to develop a coordinated strategy with other agencies to educate the public about the discrimination protections in IRCA.

"Unneccessary" Employer Burden

Have employer sanctions resulted in an unnecessary regulatory burden for employers? GAO has interpreted Congress' intent as follows: if the objectives of employer sanctions are realized, then the burden of completing the I-9 form is not "unnecessary." Conversely, if it is found that unauthorized alien employment and migration has not been reduced, it may be concluded the burden was "unnecessary." When Congress mandated that all 7 million employers complete a new form for each new hire, it expected certain benefits to come from that process. To try and measure those benefits, data on various indicators of the law's effectiveness in reducing alien employment and migration as well as the cost in time to employers to prepare the forms was reported. For example, alien apprehensions at the border, the number of nonimmigrants who overstay their visas, and the number of aliens issued nonwork social security numbers who are working were tracked. It was also reported that 10 minutes was the average time for employers to complete the I-9 form. Unfortunately, the data in the second report were inconclusive. However, it is quite likely that three years is not sufficient time to determine this law's effects on illegal migration.

THIRD REPORT PREPARATION

To answer whether the law has been implemented satisfactorily, GAO will put less emphasis on INS educational efforts and begin to concentrate on enforcement in the third and final report. Specifically, how does INS select the employers it investigates? Are industries that are known to employ most of the unauthorized aliens receiving greater attention? How useful of a deterrent has INS' program been to randomly select employers for inspection? Are there other more effective methods for targeting employers that have not been used? GAO will have audit teams in five cities (Miami, New York, Chicago, Dallas and Los Angeles) examining these issues.

To measure discrimination caused by this law, several major new initiatives have been planned. First, GAO will interview persons across the country who have recently applied for a job, and compare the way in which employers treat the Hispanics and Asians interviewed versus whites and blacks. For example, will only the Hispanics and Asians be asked to show documents? Will only the Hispanics and Asians have to complete the I-9 before being offered the job? Will persons who present work authorization documents that have a future expiration date be told the job is not available? Hopefully, many legalized aliens, refugees and asylees will be included in the universe of job applicants since it is possible they are at greatest risk of being discriminated against.

Plans have been made to do a time series analysis of EEOC national origin discrimination complaints filed from 1980 to the present. The objective is to determine if there has been a significant change in the complaints since 1986. Of course, it is important to recognize that factors other than employer sanctions could explain a change in the data.

Another survey will be sent to employers selected at random that will contain several new questions to measure discriminatory behaviors. The survey will also ask many of the same questions asked last year, but several have been changed to eliminate any possible employer confusion. For example, employers may have misinterpreted the question about beginning a policy to hire only U.S. citizens to include anyone that had work authorization documents. To avoid this problem, the term "citizen" is not used. Rather, the question has been rephrased to ask about policies to hire only persons "born in the United States."

In addition, GAO will continue to monitor the number of complaints filed with 1) the OSC, 2) the various immigrant rights organizations around the country who have set up "hotlines" to receive discrimination complaints and 3) several state and local task forces.

Although statistics from these various methods will be generated, the bottom line is that Congress did not quantify what it meant by a widespread pattern of discrimination. As a result, GAO will have to make a difficult judgment call when issuing the third report later this year. Although, at this time, it is hard to determine a conclusion, it can be assured that GAO has tried every possible legal method to get Congress the information it needs to decide whether this law should remain on the books.

FOOTNOTE:

[1] The author wishes to acknowledge the excellent cooperation his staff has received from the INS. From Commissioner Nelson and all support staff GAO has had unparalleled access to INS people and documents. This has made GAO's job immeasurably easier and Commissioner Nelson is personally thanked.

19

Assessing the Effects of IRCA's Employer Requirements and Sanctions[1]

GEORGES VERNEZ

Co-Director, Program for Research on Immigration Policy

Following in the steps of most Western European countries, in 1986 the U.S. Congress enacted the Immigration Reform and Control Act (IRCA) containing several provisions aimed at reducing illegal immigration to this country.[2] These provisions are often referred to in aggregate as "employer sanctions": They 1) prohibit all employers in the nation from hiring undocumented workers; 2) require all employers to complete an employment eligibility verification form (I-9) for each new employee; and 3) provide for graduated civil and criminal penalties for employers of undocumented workers. Accounting for concerns that employers might not hire "foreign-looking" documented workers for fear of being sanctioned, Congress also enacted a provision prohibiting employers with four or more employees from discriminating in recruitment, hiring, or discharging on the basis of a person's national origin or citizenship status. Enforcement of this provision is assigned to a newly created Office of Special Counsel (OSC) in the Justice Department.

The employer sanctions provisions of IRCA, like many of its other provisions, were created in controversy. Supporters assuming that the immigrants' predominant, if not exclusive, motivation for migration is economic, sought to remove their motivation to enter the country illegally by making it illegal to hire undocumented workers. Opponents questioned the anticipated effectiveness of this "policing" approach to illegal immigration and argued it would lead to widespread discrimination in spite of IRCA's outlawing of such practices. Because of this controversy, it is not surprising to witness a tendency by supporters and opponents alike to rush to conclusions that the provisions are having their desired or feared effects. This tendency from both sides should be resisted for several reasons.

First, the law is young. Less than two-and-a-half years have passed since IRCA was signed into law, a relatively short time, considering that millions of employers and employees have to be informed about it, understand it, and adjust their behavior accordingly. Second, IRCA's various provisions (*e.g.*, legalization, enforcement of the employer requirements, and increase in border patrol enforcements) are being implemented over a five-year period, and a lot of learning is taking place as things move along. Indeed, IRCA has given the Immigration and Naturalization Service (INS) several new and additional responsibilities for which it had no previous experience and there is evidence that the two compete (at least in the short-run) for scarce managerial and staff resources. Third, it is difficult to isolate the effects of individual provisions because they have interactive influences on the behavior of employers and of illegal immigrants.

Under the circumstances, it is not surprising that there are no clear answers about the effects of employer sanctions on illegal immigration, discrimination, and employers. When substantive pieces of the law are not in place, definitive assessments of its effects can hardly be made. At best, a few observations about the implementation status of IRCA's employer requirements and sanctions can be made. The four implementation issues related to IRCA — voluntary compliance, the phasing-in of enforcement, documentation requirements and equity of enforcement — will be briefly discussed.

COMPLIANCE

Congress expected that employers would generally comply voluntarily after being informed about the law and understanding its multiple provisions. Available evidence suggests that voluntary compliance is at the half-way mark, as far as filing I-9 forms and inspecting workers' documents are concerned. According to a General Accounting Office (GAO) survey of more than 6,000 employees throughout the nation, 50 percent of employers surveyed who knew about the I-9 requirements were fully complying.[3] This survey and a survey of employers in New York in 1988 indicate that 78 to 87 percent of employers knew about the employer sanctions under IRCA.[4] For Fiscal Year 1988, the Department of Labor's I-9 audits indicate that 57 percent of the firms it inspected fully or partially complied.[5]

Noncompliance seems to be correlated with administrative problems and misunderstanding about I-9 verification requirements. Evidence suggests that it may be related to employers' perceptions of the sanction threat and how difficult it is for them to find authorized workers. In turn, employers' knowledge of and compliance with IRCA's provisions seem to be correlated with firm size and whether they were visited or contacted by the INS. Thus, voluntary compliance can be expected to increase as the INS makes more contacts with employers and employers become more aware and knowledgeable about the law. A new GAO survey being fielded in the Spring of 1989 will be instructive in this regard.

So far, the indications are that employers do not perceive IRCA's requirements as a major burden. Large companies see them as "just one more government regulation"; it would be uncharacteristic if they didn't. However, the requirements may not have generated any outcry because enforcement has not yet been very widespread and rigorous.

PHASING-IN ENFORCEMENT

INS is currently implementing the second of what may become a four-phase employer enforcement strategy.

Phase I was the "education" phase. As Congress intended, this phase lasted from December 1987 to June 1988. The first six months were to be a public education period, followed by a 12-month period during which citations would be issued for first-time violations. Thus, in the early stages of IRCA's implementation (lasting through June 1988), the INS declared itself in an "educational mode," approaching this new function in a cooperative spirit[6] and sought voluntary compliance rather than issuing citations.[7] During that period more than 50 percent of INS investigative time and a sizable proportion of border patrol resources were allocated to educating employers.[8] The INS contacted about 1 million employers in person or by phone and sent out more than 7 million booklets. INS had established a goal of 20,000 inspections for Fiscal Year 1988. It completed about 12,000 in that time; fewer than 2,000 employers were cited and 100 were given "intent-to-file" (ITF) citations.

Phase II, the current phase, began in July 1988, when the law allowed INS to fine for first-time violations of the law. Education continues but is mixed with slightly more aggressive enforcement. The education efforts now include information on antidiscrimination provisions, which evidently were not emphasized during Phase I. Twenty-five percent of time spent by the investigation staff is still being devoted to education and 500,000 additional employers are to be contacted. Also, and consistent with INS continuing informational efforts, a warning notice (instead of a notice of an "intent to fine") may be issued for first-time violations under specified circumstances.[9]

The number of employer investigations has held steady, rather than increasing. Through February 1989, 5,000 had been investigated. However, the emphasis has shifted from warnings to issuing ITF citations for first offenses. The latter now represent 54 percent of citations, compared with 17 percent in Phase I, and 1,250 have been issued since June 1988. Fines have been relatively small and have held steady over Phases I and II, averaging about five-thousand dollars; 20 percent of cases have been appealed and, so far, the INS has sought no criminal sanctions.

The INS has not announced plans for Phases III and IV; therefore, descriptions of the next two phases are, of course, speculative. Nevertheless, they may take the following course. Phase III could focus on vigorous enforcement of employer sanctions, through stepped-up investigations and increasingly more severe penalties. This pattern has been followed by other countries (*e.g.*, France and West Germany) that passed laws similar to IRCA in the mid-1970s.[10]

Sequentially or concurrently, Phase IV may then begin to focus on employees who use fraudulent or borrowed documents. Although it is not intrinsically an employer sanctions issue, widespread use of counterfeit documents could seriously undermine attempts to enforce sanctions against hiring undocumented workers.

DOCUMENTATION

A few limited studies suggest that up to 40 percent or more of undocumented workers who have been hired or are seeking employment have fraudulent documents which are either borrowed from friends or relatives or counterfeit (primarily Social Security or alien registration cards).[11] In addition, it is recognized that documents used for the Social Security number application and those used for employment authorization are vulnerable to fraud. To date, education of employers on document review and acceptance has been minimal. Furthermore, because so many different kinds of documents can be offered as proof of eligibility, employers have not been and cannot be expected to be educated on the large number of acceptable documents, nor can they reasonably be expected to become expert at identifying frauds.

Just as the multiplicity of acceptable documentation offers many opportunities for counterfeit and fraud, it also offers many opportunities for erroneous denial of employment. For instance, one study concludes that in spite of efforts to inform and educate employers about the law's requirements, about one in five employers surveyed in New York City in 1988 did not know about all alternative forms of authorized documentation, particularly the less frequently used types of documents such as those provided by INS to refugees and asylum applicants.[12] Ironically, it seems that reducing the number of acceptable documents may be necessary and desirable to minimize both fraud and potential discriminatory practices.

What actually happens in employer enforcement and fraud prevention will depend not only on the INS but on funds made available by the Administration and Congress. In other words, it will depend on the commitment of the nation through its legislative, executive, and judicial branches to enforcement of IRCA's intent. Federal budget constraints, and pressures to reduce the budget deficit, may well put enforcement low on the scale of priorities.

EQUITY OF ENFORCEMENT

Assuring fairness of enforcement of the employer sanctions across industries, regions, and localities is of concern to Congress. In the case of industries, inspections may be initiated in one of two ways: 1) as a result of a lead based on local information (including complaints, FBI tips, knowledge or suspicion that certain firms hire undocumented workers or records of past violations) or 2) through a selection of firms done centrally at INS headquarters in Washington, DC. Half of the firms randomly selected are to be selected from economic sectors that used to employ significant numbers of unauthorized aliens (as determined by local district management) and half from all other employers.[13] As of February 1989, 75 percent of inspections were based on leads and 25 percent were random. The intent is to eventually have 60 percent of resources devoted to the first type of inspections and 40 percent to the second.

As for regions and localities, available information suggests significant variations in the level of enforcement and in enforcement practices between INS regions and districts. The INS southern region has been much more involved in issuing ITF citations than the other three INS regions. It accounts for more than half. In that district, 50 percent of all citations were ITFs, compared to 12 to 18 percent in the other three regions.

Regional variations in enforcement strategies may result from factors both internal, as noted above, and external to INS. Local economic conditions and industry structures are two such factors. Another is the response of local prosecutors and courts. Criminal sanctions require that local district attorneys prosecute. They may be more or less aggressive in different parts of the country, depending on their workloads. Courts may also cause variations across regions. For instance, in San Francisco, a court ordered the INS to limit its searches to consent searches, or to obtain a search warrant based on probable cause before visiting a firm.

In summary, IRCA's employer requirements and sanctions are being implemented over time, and definite conclusions about the extent and nature of its effects, positive and/or negative can not yet be drawn. Nevertheless, as of 1988, one out of two employers were fully or partially complying. Of those who did not comply, nearly half were not fully aware of IRCA's requirements and eventual sanctions for noncompliance. To date in early 1989, the INS continues to be more in an "education" mode. In order to encourage compliance, INS also has begun to use the threat of sanctions more frequently. But INS has yet to increase its frequency of inspections and the average size of its fine. There is evidence of variations in enforcement among regions and districts as well.

FOOTNOTES

[1] The views expressed are the personal views of the author and are not necessarily shared by the Program for Research on Immigration Policy or its two sponsoring institutions, the RAND Corporation and The Urban Institute. Unless otherwise noted, the data presented were obtained directly from the Immigration and Naturalization Service.

[2] For a discussion of Western European experience, *See* Miller, Mark J., and Malcolm R. Lovell, Jr., *Employer Sanctions in Europe*, Center for Immigration Studies, Paper #3, April 1987.

[3] United States General Accounting Office, *Immigration Reform: Status of Implementing Employer Sanctions After Second Year*, Government Printing Office, GAO/660-89-16, November 1988.

[4] New York State Inter-Agency Task Force on Immigration Affairs, *Workplace Discrimination Under the Immigration Reform and Control Act of 1986: A Study of the Impacts on New Workers*, November 1988.

[5] Computed from data provided by the Department of Labor.

[6] John R. Schroeder, "The Immigration Reform and Control Act of 1986." In *In Defense of the Alien*, edited by Lydio F. Tomasi, Staten Island, New York: The Center for Migration Studies, 1988.

[7] United States General Accounting Office, *Immigration Reform: Status of Implementing Employer Sanctions After One Year*, Government Printing Office, GAO/660-88-14, November 1987.

[8] The involvement of the border patrol in educating employers about their new IRCA requirements and in enforcing them was unanticipated by Congress. Still, one out of three citations and ITF notices have been issued by border patrol agents nationwide.

[9] In general, "specified circumstances," are interpreted to mean that if the employer had not received an educational or other INS visit and there were no egregious factors present such as willful failure to complete I-9s or willful hiring of undocumented workers.

[10] Miller, Mark J. and Malcolm R. Lovell, Jr., *Ibid.*

[11] United States General Accounting Office, *Ibid*, 1988, and Wayne Cornelius, *The Persistence of Immigrant-Dominated Firms and Industries in the United States: The Case of California*, paper prepared for the Conference on Comparative Migration Studies in Paris, June 1988.

[12] New York State Inter-Agency Task Force on Immigration Affairs, *Ibid.*

[13] United States General Accounting Office, *Ibid*, November 1988.

20

Assessing the Impact of IRCA'S Employer Sanctions Provisions

MICHAEL C. LEMAY

Frostburg State University, Frostburg, Maryland

The 1980s saw a strongly renewed interest in immigration policy surface in the United States. After more than half a decade of strenuous debate, the United States Congress finally passed, in October of 1986, the Immigration Reform and Control Act (IRCA). It was signed into law by President Reagan on November 6, 1986. Aptly described as one of the great social experiments of our time, it represents the most significant shift in the nation's immigration policy and law in 35 years.[1]

As recently as the summer before its passage, IRCA seemed to be an issue for which the proposal was "a corpse going to the morgue."[2] Senator Simpson, its sponsor, had reintroduced the bill, which the Senate passed for a third time in September,1985. The House once again left the bill open to tinkering by submitting its version of the bill to six committees.

The Judiciary Committee seemed deadlocked over the farmworker provision. It did not complete its drafting of the bill until the end of June, and then five other committees worked on it throughout the summer. When the House, late in September of 1986, rejected a rule for considering a bill (HR 3810), immigration reform seemed indeed a dead issue.[3]

A small group of House members long involved with the issue refused to let it die. Led by Representative Charles E. Schumer (D-NY), they put the pieces back together again. Representative Rodino, chair of the Judiciary Committee, and Hamilton Fish, Jr., its ranking Republican, aided Schumer in crafting a compromise. Schumer met with representative Howard Berman (D-CA), and Leon Panetta (D-CA) and the three hammered out a key aspect of the new compromise — the temporary farmworkers provision. Extensive discussion with Representative Lungren (R-CA), the ranking Republican, and Romano Mazzoli, the chair of the Judiciary Immigration, Refugees and International Law Subcommittee, resulted in further fine tuning of the bill's provisions. After House members agreed on the new package, including numerous points designed to protect the rights of the temporary workers, they secured Senator Simpson's support as well.

In 1986, Congress was in a better mood to pass an immigration law than in any previous year. As the Mexican economy deteriorated late in 1985 and early 1986, and the peso plunged in value, the INS caught a record number of illegal aliens attempting to cross. Their apprehensions rose by 31 percent during the fiscal year — to 1.8 million (See Figure 1). The growing conservative mood of the country seemed to convince liberal opponents of the bill that continued resistance would only lead to even stricter legislation in 1987.

A key shift, enabling passage of the bill, came when the Hispanic Caucus split on the bill, with five members supporting and six opposing. That split also enabled the Black Congressional Caucus to split on the bill. Representative Robert Garcia (D-NY) and Edward Roybal (D-CA) continued to lead those who opposed the bill. Representative Esteban Torres (D-CA), chair of the Hispanic Caucus, and Albert Bustamente (D-TX), vice-chairman, both voted for the bill.

The compromise on the temporary farmworker provision negotiated by Representative Schumer also split the opposition to the bill among the Western fruit and vegetable growers. His compromise served to meet the demands among growers for foreign workers while allowing for sufficient protection of the workers against likely exploitation so as to win over enough of the Hispanic, liberal, and union votes in Congress to allow passage of the bill. Representative Schumer described the new bill as "a left-center bill," in contrast to the "right-center" version killed by the House Democrats in 1984. In 1984, House Democrats opposed it by a margin of 183 to 125. In the October, 1986 vote, Democrats supported it by a vote of 168 to 61. The House passed the new compromise version on October 9, 1986 by a margin of 230 to 166.[4]

Passage by the House once again necessitated a Conference Committee to make adjustments between the two differing versions. Six issues remained in significant conflict: 1) The House version terminated employer penalties automatically after six and one-half years. The Senate version and the administration vigorously opposed that House bill's provision; 2) The House version contained an amendment sponsored by Representative Joseph Moakley (D-MA), that granted temporary legal status to Salvadorans and Nicaraguans who were here illegally. The White House and the State Department strongly objected to that provision. 3) The House version had a provision by Barney Frank (D-MA) that barred an employer from discrimi-

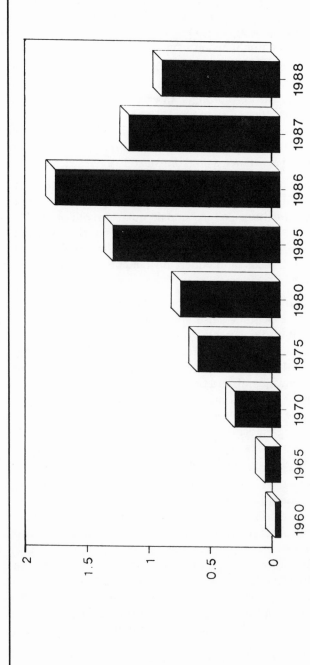

FIGURE 1
INS APPREHENSIONS AT U.S. BORDERS
1960-1988

Source: Adapted from graph and data in: GAO, Immigration Reform: Status of Implementing Employer Sanctions After One Year, November, 1987. Washington D.C.: U.S. Government Printing Office, 1987:8; with 1987 data added, from U.S. Dept. of Justice, INS Reporter, January, 1988 Washington, D.C.: U.S. Government Printing Office 1988:21; and updated to 1988 by INS data cited in "Border Attacks Worry INS Agents," The Washington Post, October 16, 1988:A-18.

nating in hiring on the basis of citizenship and creating a Special Counsel in the Justice Department to investigate such alleged discrimination; this provision was opposed by both the Senate and the administration; 4) The two versions differed in the dates for starting the "legalization" program, the House version set the eligibility date at January 1, 1982; the Senate version granted amnesty to those aliens here prior to January 1, 1980; 5) The two versions differed over how the federal government would reimburse states for costs associated with the complex legalization program, the House version provided for 100 percent federal reimbursement, the Senate bill provided for 3 billion dollars over the six years after enactment; 6) The House bill included a provision sponsored by Howard Berman (D-CA) that provided free legal services to farmworkers entering the country under the H-2 temporary worker program.

The 1986 Conference Committee agreed upon a series of compromises to settle those six issues. The House agreed to the Senate version without the automatic end to sanctions in exchange for Senate provisions requiring Congress to review the program within three years, at which time the program could be terminated by joint resolution if the comptroller general determined that the employer sanction program had resulted in discrimination. The House also agreed to give up the Moakley provisions on Salvadorans and Nicaraguans in return for an administration pledge not to deport any Salvadorans to areas stricken by an October, 1986 earthquake. In addition, Chairman Rodino promised to consider a bill on the subject early in the 100th Congress, and Senator Simpson promised that he would not prevent Senate consideration of such a bill if it passed the House. The Senate agreed to accept the Frank antidiscrimination provisions, and accepted in slightly modified form, the free legal representation for H-2 workers. It was understood that such legal work would apply only to job-related problems such as wages, hours and work conditions. The funding issue was resolved with a one billion dollar appropriation for the next four years, with unspent money in one year being available in the following year. Any unused money at the end of Fiscal Year 1990 could be carried over through Fiscal Year 1994. The compromise funding version further specified that the amount of government payments for Social Security supplements and Medicaid would be deducted from the one billion dollar appropriation. Finally, the Senate agreed to the House version of the amnesty program's starting date of January 1, 1982.

The bill's tangled history helped make these compromises possible in 1986. Increased concern with the immigration problem meant that nearly everyone involved wanted a bill of some kind to pass. Previous disagreements meant that there was less need for "political posturing." Congress desperately wanted to recess for the up-coming elections. In the words of Representative

Mazzoli, "It's not a perfect bill, but its the least imperfect bill we will ever have before us."[5]

The House passed the measure by a vote of 238-173 on Wednesday, October 15, 1986. The Senate approved it by a vote of 63-24 on Friday, October 17, 1986. President Reagan signed the bill into law on November 6, 1986.

Assessing the Impact of IRCA

Assessing the effectiveness of IRCA is at best a difficult task.[6] As a *Time* magazine feature on immigration noted, the debate over the immigration bills was drawn out, convoluted, and acrimonious. Yet as *Time* succinctly put it:

> That is perhaps as it should be. Seldom has so important an issue come so far so often in the legislative process with those concerned with it having so little idea of its potential effects. No one can say for sure whether immigration reform can be made to work, what it might cost and, most important, whether it would ultimately help or hurt the country. In that information vacuum, politicians, businessmen, labor leaders, minority representatives and social scientists have taken positions on all sides of the issue. President Reagan is maintaining a discreet profile, hoping only for a policy that is "fair and nondiscriminatory" (July 8, 1985).

IRCA, as most laws that attempt to set a new direction in public policy, seems to have achieved less impact on the flow of illegal immigrants into this country than its proponents had hoped, but it has also had less discriminatory effect upon minorities than its critics had feared.

This first assessment of IRCA must be rather tentatively made as there has been a rather short duration, to date, within which to measure its impact. Also, commonly accepted empirical indicators of its effects are lacking. At this point in time the analysis must remain largely descriptive and simplistic. Further scholarly analysis is needed before a consensus of the appropriate indicators of the law's impact may be achieved.

The following discussion will be limited to the employer sanctions provisions of IRCA.

EMPLOYER SANCTIONS

Before the passage of IRCA, the act's proponents viewed employment as the magnet drawing aliens here and that the employer sanctions provisions were designed to close the job market to undocumented workers. The major controversy with these provisions centered on a fear that such sanctions would lead to widespread discrimination against authorized aliens and even native-born Americans who appeared "foreign" (principally Hispanic-

Americans). To address these concerns IRCA makes it illegal to discriminate against any individual on account of national origin or citizenship status; however, it is not illegal to select a U.S. citizen over an alien for employment if the two are equally qualified. In addition, an Office of Special Counsel (OSC) was established to investigate and prosecute charges of immigration-related employment discrimination. In the event that these measures proved ineffective and there is evidence of widespread discrimination to be determined by a series of reports by the General Accounting Office (GAO), then the employer sanctions program can be terminated after three years.

The optimistic assessment of the ability of the employer sanction method for cutting down on illegal immigration holds that such sanctions are essential to cutting off the illegal immigrant flow. Initial reaction to IRCA and to confusion over the rules adopted by the Immigration and Naturalization Service (INS) to implement the law have led to some instances indicating abuses involving the exploitation of undocumented workers.[7] There are indications that some employers are, indeed, voluntarily complying with the law and actively cooperating with the INS. Other employers, however, are clearly willing to break the law. Elaborate smuggling and phony documentation schemes have developed to circumvent the law.[8]

Can the impact of IRCA's employer sanctions provisions, in a manner that goes beyond merely impressionistic incidents reported by the mass media be assessed? In short, can it be determined whether or not a "widespread pattern of discrimination" is in any way evident? Several such indicators are possible.

Figure 1, shows the annual number of apprehensions of illegal entrants at the U.S. borders since 1960. The numbers rose steadily until passage of IRCA. In the first year after the act's passage, such numbers dropped off by a fairly impressive 30 percent. In Fiscal Year 1988, the INS caught 940,670 illegal aliens, a drop of 16 percent from the previous year and a 42 percent decline from the pre-IRCA 1986 figure.[9] These data are graphically shown in Figure 2, where the trend line demonstrates a dramatic drop-off in the first few months after passage of IRCA. This trend, however, has begun to reverse, climb again and start to approximate the form of the year prior to passage of IRCA. As economic pressures in Mexico and other Central and South American nations induce a northern flow and as initial fear of IRCA employer sanctions provisions wear off or are simply seen to be easily avoided through the acquisition of false documents, making employment readily possible again, the number of illegal entrants seized can be expected to rise again, perhaps near to pre-IRCA levels.

The employer sanctions provision essentially makes the employer an immigration agent. But the lack of a clear method to ensure proper documentation leaves the employer on the horns of a dilemma. Under-zealous

FIGURE 2

APPREHENSIONS AT U.S. BORDERS, BY MONTH
MAY, 1986 TO MAY, 1988

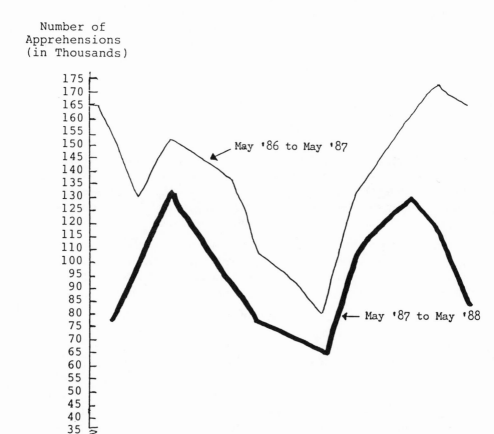

Source: Graph adapted by author from data and graph in U.S. Department of Justice, INS Reporter.
Washington, D.C.: U.S. Government Printing Office, January 1988:21.

compliance could lead to fines and penalties being imposed. Yet over-zeal-ousness could lead to massive civil rights violations of due process and the citizens' rights to privacy. The new law is likely to develop a whole new line of case and administrative law from complaints by racial and ethnic groups of discrimination against employers instead of the INS.[10]

The INS's enforcement approach began with an emphasis on education and voluntary compliance — an effort to establish a foundation for phasing in enforcement actions against employers who willfully violate the law. The first citation was issued in August 1987 and the first notice of Intent to Fine was served in October 1987. As of February 19, 1988, a total of 1,334 citations and 40 Notices of Intent to Fine had been issued. The first such prosecution under IRCA's employer sanctions provisions involved the Wendy's fast food chains in the Washington, D.C. area. Their parent corporation, DavCoFood Inc. of Crofton, Maryland, which operates Wendy's in the capital, Maryland and northern Virginia, agreed to pay a sixty-thousand dollar fine. To assess the overall level of compliance, the INS is currently implementing an inspec-tion program for which employers are randomly selected.[11]

Insofar as employer sanctions fail to deter the employer, they are not likely to reduce illegal immigration. Far from reducing the number of such illegal aliens, the new law may ironically create a double "criminalization" of undocu-mented workers. To get a job the immigrant will have to cross the border without papers and will also have to present the employer with bogus documents. Such workers will thus be even more vulnerable and potentially more susceptible to implicit or explicit blackmail by their employers. It is, indeed, predictable that the undocumented workers, and in some cases even the documented ones, will pay a price for the IRCA approach to immigration policy. As the release of pertinent data makes it possible to do in the near future, IRCA will have to be assessed as to its effect on such factors as layoffs, wage reductions, and perhaps even up-front payments at the time of employment. Employees will pay for the greater "risk" their employers assume in hiring them.

Figure 2, shows that after a fall-off in the number of apprehensions of 42 percent in the first few months after IRCA was enacted, the numbers rose again in a manner very parallel to previous years, if not to the same level.

An initial indication of whether or not IRCA has led to a pattern of widespread discrimination is presented in Table 1. Critics of the law argued that employer sanctions would tend to reduce the number of jobs and/or the wage levels in those occupations where the illegal aliens had traditionally found jobs. The table shows data on job and personal income levels in selected job categories for California, Florida and Texas. If any widespread pattern of discrimination were evident because of the passage of IRCA it would first show up in these states. Table 1 shows the percent change from

TABLE 1

ECONOMIC ANALYSIS OF JOB DISCRIMINATION FOR SELECTED STATES AND JOB CATEGORIES PERCENT CHANGE PRE- TO POST-IRCA

STATE	JOB DATA		
	Percent Change in Full- and Part-Time Employment/ Farm Sector for Selected Years:		
	1984 to 1985	1985 to 1986	1986 to 1987
CA	−.022	−.018	.011
FLA	−.048	.023	−.018
TX	−.053	−.094	.036
	Percent Change, Mixed Farm Labor Expense		
CA	.003	−.009	.084
FL	−.002	−.003	.075
TX	.005	−.034	.078
	PERSONAL INCOME DATA		
	Farm Personal Income		
	1984 to 1985	1985 to 1986	1986 to 1987
CA	−.10	.10	−.09
FL	.07	−.10	.02
TX	.04	−.006	.02
	Agricultural Services, Forestry, Fishing, Other		
CA	.04	.11	.04
FL	.09	.04	.28
TX	.04	−.006	.02
	Services		
CA	.12	.09	.09
FL	.12	.10	.13
TX	.08	.04	.07

Source: Department of Commerce, Bureau of Economic Analysis User's Group at Frostburg State University, Table SA 25 "Full- and Part-Time Employees by Industry," Table SA 5, "Personal Income by Major Source."

1984 to 1985, from 1985 to 1986, and from 1986 to 1987 in full- and part-time employment in the farm sectors. It further reports the percent change in mixed farm labor expenses. Finally, it looks at personal income data in three job categories which would most register any such change in response to IRCA: farm personal income, income in "agricultural service, forestry, fishing and other," and personal income for "services." The percent changes in all cases for all years in all three states is miniscule. Clearly, these data suggest that there is no widespread pattern of discrimination causing significant changes in wage or employment levels, as critics feared, in precisely those areas that would be most susceptible to IRCA's impact.

The flow of illegal immigration responds not only to the opportunity of job availability which "draws" people to the U.S., but also to economic and political pressures that "push" people to leave their countries of origin.

The Mexican population is growing exponentially — at an annual rate of 3.2 percent compared to the 0.9 percent annual growth rate of the United States. Mexican per capita income is seven hundred forty dollars, while the U.S. annual per capita income is over six thousand dollars. Demographic projections estimate that Mexico will double its population every 20 years, reaching 150 million by the turn of the century. The political instability in Central America will clearly continue to push migration northward, further increasing pressure on Mexico. Clearly, it will become increasingly attractive to cross the Rio Grande, legally or illegally, and work for whatever wages are available, as even the lowest U.S. wages will be far above those in Mexico. Mexican legislators predict that as time passes, IRCA will increasingly fail to stem the flow northward and may further strain U.S./Mexican, and possibly even U.S./Canadian, relations.[12]

IRCA represents a compromise that allows for the reinforcement of anti-immigrant sentiment, while avoiding any substantial change in the economic and political realities that propel the immigrant to seek employment in the U.S.

The extent to which discrimination has been increased or not by passage of IRCA has also been addressed by GAO. The GAO has been specifically charged with reporting back to Congress in November of 1987, 1988, and 1989 on the impact of IRCA in general, and on this aspect of the law in particular. In its second annual report on IRCA, dated November 15, 1988, the GAO noted that there were 286 discrimination charges filed with the OSC as of September 19, 1988 and that 148 such charges were filed with the Equal Employment Opportunity Commission (EEOC) as of September 15, 1988. Of these charges, 54 were filed with both agencies. Excluding duplicate charges, the total such charges are 340. Additionally, EEOC identified 15 IRCA-related charges filed with state and local human rights agencies.

As of October, 1988, an administrative law judge had rendered one discrimination-related decision (*Romo* v. *Todd Corporation*). The judge ruled that
the employee failed to qualify as a protected individual under IRCA's citizenship status discrimination provision even though the judge stated that
the employee was wrongfully fired. (*See* GAO Report, November, 1988:41).
Moreover, since charges filed with the OSC may not be solely the result of
employer sanctions, all charges cannot be used in deciding whether or not a
pattern of discrimination is evident. The GAO reviewed all 119 charges filed
with the OSC as of May, 1988. Of the 119 charges, 62 involved persons who
were fired, 48 involved persons who were not hired, and the remaining 9
charges related to other issues. The GAO determined 19 of 119 cases did not
appear to be related to employer sanctions, and in 34 cases it was unable to
determine whether the charges were related to employer sanctions because
of insufficient data . Of the 66 charges that appeared to relate specifically to
employer sanctions, 33 alleged the employer refused to accept authorized
work documents. Of the 66 sanctions-related charges, 34 are still under
investigation and 32 were closed; 9 of 32 were closed with no reason to believe
the charge was true, 14 were closed with settlement; and 9 were closed
because the OSC lacked jurisdiction.

Likewise, with the EEOC-filed charges, a total of 148 were made for
various reasons. The GAO reviewed 38 IRCA-related charges. Of these, GAO
classified 14 charges as appearing to be employer sanctions-related, and 7 as
unrelated. The GAO was unable to classify the other 17 charges.

Besides these data, the GAO examined charges filed with other federal,
state and local agencies and private organizations. These included the Department of Labor (DOL), the INS, several state and local human rights
agencies, and public interest groups that assist immigrants. Little additional
evidence of discrimination emerged from this data. For example, the DOL
inspected employers' I-9 forms to look for evidence of "disparate treatment."
The GAO reviewed 4,130 ESA-I-9 forms at the INS' district offices in the five
highest alien population cities and found that the DOL marked a mere 3 such
forms as showing "disparate treatment."

Following the GAO's initial report in November, 1987, the INS undertook
several suggested actions to educate the public as well as its own officials
about IRCA's antidiscrimination provisions. The INS is working with OSC
and DOL to develop a comprehensive education program.

The GAO also surveyed 104 state and local human rights agencies that
enforce antidiscrimination laws to assess the extent to which they were aware
of IRCA's relevant provisions. Of 81 responses, 30 indicated they were greatly
or very greatly familiar with IRCA's provisions and 7 said they were not
familiar. Thirty-seven indicated they did not have OSC's address and 42 did

not have its toll-free telephone number. Forty-four lacked the OSC form to file discrimination charges. A mere 6 reported they had referred a complaint to the OSC. Fifty-nine said they had received information about IRCA's antidiscrimination provisions from EEOC. Thirty-four of the responding agencies stated that IRCA's provisions could conflict with their anti-discrimination laws. Additionally, five EEOC district offices reported 15 IRCA-related charges had been filed with state and local agencies.

The GAO report also discussed its contact with the Center for Immigrant Rights which operates an employer sanctions telephone line to collect complaints of IRCA-related discrimination and abuse. From June, 1988 to August, 1988 the Center received 18 calls alleging specific IRCA-related hiring complaints. The Center also received 45 calls concerning work-place abuse. The Center believes, moreover, such instances of reported problems understate the extent of discrimination because workers have not yet been educated about their rights, do not recognize discrimination, do not know where to seek redress, or are simply too frightened to complain.

Similarly, the Mexican American Legal Defense and Educational Fund (MALDEF) was consulted by the GAO. They reported that a Los Angeles based coalition concerned with immigration reform had received 194 complaints about IRCA-related discrimination between November 1986 and September, 1988. The types of complaints included: penalizing employees for previous use of false documents or aliases; requiring work documents of grandfathered individuals who were not authorized to work; accusing employees of using fraudulent documents that were valid; and favoring U.S. citizens over noncitizens. According to the project report, in 73 of the cases the employers demanded more documents than the law requires or requested specific documents that the law does not permit. Forty-four of the cases were filed with OSC, EEOC, state or local antidiscrimination agencies, unions or other organizations. In addition to the 194 cases in Los Angeles, MALDEF's Chicago office provided data on 58 discrimination charges filed there from April, 1987 to August, 1988.

The GAO report cites data from the City of Chicago's Commission on Human Relations which as of July 31, 1988 had received 122 alleged IRCA discrimination-related charges. Of the 122 charges, the Commission resolved 63, had 13 under investigation, and referred 46 to other agencies. Likewise, the State of Illinois Department of Human Rights had 8 IRCA- related charges filed as of August 31, 1988. The Commission also reiterated the point that this number did not represent the true scope of the unlawful discrimination problems caused by IRCA since many immigrants still fear government officials and are reluctant to come forward to seek relief.

Similarly, the New York State Assembly Task Force on New Americans sponsored a public hearing on November 2, 1987 to assess the effects of employer sanctions in New York. During the hearings several advocacy groups and individuals gave testimonial evidence of sanctions leading to intimidation and unnecessary firings, which included: fear of sanctions leading to discrimination against legal immigrants, employer ignorance of acceptable documents, discrimination against U.S. citizens (especially Puerto Ricans since many employers do not know that Puerto Ricans are indeed U.S. citizens), employers of IRCA (especially those assisting undocumented employees with their legalization applications), and charges that the INS has not yet done an adequate job of educating employers about IRCA's sanction and antidiscrimination provisions.

The GAO concluded in its 1988 report that the data on discrimination does not establish 1) a pattern of discrimination caused by employer sanctions or 2) an unreasonable burden on employers (1988:4).

In short, as all these data indicate that the total number of charges, while undoubtedly underreported, nonetheless has been in the range of only several hundreds. That is certainly quite different from the "widespread pattern of discrimination" that some of IRCA's critics had feared and predicted. In comparison, when the EEOC was first created to deal with job discrimination — granted in a broader context and for which more grounds to base charges existed — it received 8,196 complaints in 1966 during its first full year of operation (EEOC, Annual Report, 1967).

In its first annual report, however, the GAO added a caveat worth noting here:

> Determining the extent of discrimination caused by employers' fear of sanctions is also difficult. . .There will be no data on the number of persons who applied for the estimated 67.5 million jobs filled in a given year who were not hired because of employers' fears of sanctions. Without this information, it may not be possible for us to determine what is a "widespread pattern" of discrimination versus "no significant" discrimination. Given these difficulties, we have devised an indicator to test whether employers' fear of sanctions may cause discrimination. . .employers are required to file the I-9 form for new hires except when state employment agencies agree to certify the individuals' employment eligibility. In such cases, if INS later determines the persons are unauthorized workers, the employer cannot be sanctioned for hiring them unless INS can prove the employer did not act in good faith. We plan to compare the placement rates of different ethnic groups between state employment agencies that provide certificates and those agencies that do not. Significant differences between

the two may provide an indication of the effect that fear of sanctions had on the hiring among ethnic groups and therefore may indicate discrimination (1987:4, 32).

In its 1988 Report, the GAO reported on the results of its survey data which did, indeed, indicate some degree of unfair employment practices (1988: 46-53). The survey showed that two major provisions in the law, with respect to discrimination, were clearly not well understood (as had been often charged by the nongovernmental agencies cited above). Of the estimated 1.7 million employers who were aware of and reviewed information on IRCA, the GAO estimated that approximately 20 percent (around 332,000) were unclear about the authority to hire a U.S. citizen rather than an authorized alien when both are equally qualified, and that 1 percent (about 248,000) were unclear about the penalties for employers who discriminate. In addition, the survey indicated that about 16 percent (an estimated 528,000) of the 3.3 million employers who were aware of the law reported beginning or increasing policies or practices that may not be permitted under the law. For example, some employers stated that they 1) asked only foreign-looking or foreign-sounding job applicants for work authorization documents, 2) asked only current workers who were foreign-looking or foreign-sounding to present work authorization documents, and 3) began a new policy to hire only U.S. citizens.

The GAO survey found that unfair hiring practices were generally not related to the employers' state of residence, industry, or size of business. Instead, they seem to be most related to the employers' knowledge of IRCA's I-9 verification requirements and previous INS visits. Also, those employers who responded that they had fired grandfathered employees for not having work authorization documents were located in the five high alien population states. While the number of respondents who said they had begun or increased these unfair practices because of employer sanctions is too small for the GAO to project to the entire population of U.S. employers, most of the employers who did report beginning or increasing such unfair practices indicated they did so because of IRCA's sanctions. These data are graphically shown in Figure 3.

The lack of a consistent pattern of unfair hiring practices existing between the five high alien population states and industries and other states and industries, and the lack of a consistent pattern of such unfair labor practices and the number of employees are shown in Tables 2, 3, and 4.

CONCLUSION

The author has been highly critical elsewhere of the basic approach of IRCA (*See* LeMay, 1986, 1987, 1989). This initial assessment of IRCA, however, seems

FIGURE 3

EMPLOYERS USING UNFAIR HIRING POLICIES/PRACTICES

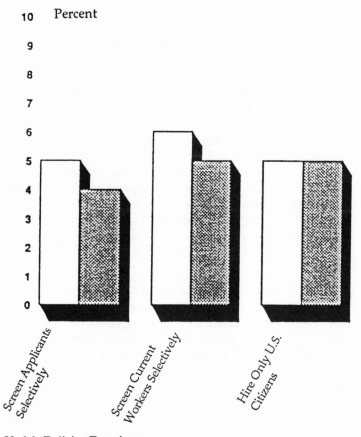

Unfair Policies/Practices

☐ Using unfair policies/practices

▨ Using such policies/practices because of employer sanctions

Note: N = 3,169

Source: GAO Employer Survey, Spring, 1988, "Report to Congress: Immigration Reform," General Accounting Office, November, 1988:48.

TABLE 2
EMPLOYER RESPONSE TO UNFAIR PRACTICES BY STATE

Type of unfair employment practice	Employers by states					
	CA	FL	TX	NY	IL	Other
Screen job applicants selectively						
Universe	519,000	216,000	369,000	252,000	197,000	1,316,000
Respondents[a,b]	53,000	29,000	16,000	30,000	20,000	66,000
Percentage	10	13	4	12	10	5
Screen current workers selectively						
Universe	506,000	211,000	369,000	249,000	196,000	1,316,000
Respondents[a,c]	78,000	20,000	16,000	25,000	22,000	82,000
Percentage	15	9	4	10	11	6
Hire only U.S. citizens						
Universe	515,000	212,000	352,000	249,000	195,000	1,304,000
Respondents[a]	73,000	23,000	38,000	13,000	22,000	110,000
Percentage	14	11	11	5	11	8

[a] These are estimates.
[b] These employers responded that they began or increased asking only foreign-looking or -sounding job applicants to prove they were authorized workers.
[c] These employers responded that they began or increased examining work authorization documents of only foreign-looking or -sounding current workers.

Source: *Ibid*, GAO Report to Congress, 1988:49.

TABLE 3

EMPLOYER RESPONSES TO UNFAIR EMPLOYMENT PRACTICES, BY INDUSTRY

Type of unfair employment practice	Employers by industry					
	Construction	Farming	Food processing	Garment	Hotel/ restaurant	Other
Screen job applicants selectively						
Universe	208,000	39,000	9,000	8,000	92,000	2,513,000
Respondents[a,b]	12,000	5,000	1,000	1,000	12,000	183,000
Percent	6	13	11	13	13	7
Screen current workers selectively						
Universe	212,000	39,000	9,000	8,000	90,000	2,489,000
Respondents[a,c]	18,000	5,000	1,000	1,000	10,000	208,000
Percent	8	13	11	13	11	8
Hire only U.S. citizens						
Universe	207,000	38,000	9,000	8,000	90,000	2,477,000
Respondents[a]	27,000	3,000	1,000	1,000	9,000	239,000
Percent	13	8	11	13	10	10

[a] These are estimates. •
[b] These employers responded that they began or increased asking only foreign-looking or -sounding job applicants to prove they were authorized workers.
[c] These employers responded that they began or increased examining work authorization documents of only foreign-looking or -sounding current workers.

Source: *Ibid*: 50.

TABLE 4

EMPLOYER RESPONSES TO UNFAIR EMPLOYMENT PRACTICES
BY NUMBER OF EMPLOYEES

Type of Unfair	Number of Employees			
Employment Practice	1-3[a]	4-9	10-50	51 or more
Screen Job Applicants Selectively				
Universe	743,000	825,000	825,000	314,000
Respondents[b,c]	41,000	69,000	89,000	6,000
Percent	6	8	11	2
Screen Current Workers Selectively				
Universe	742,000	809,000	821,000	313,000
Respondents[b]	45,000	65,000	100,000	22,000
Percent	6	8	12	7
Hire Only U.S. Citizen				
Universe	736,000	807,000	812,000	308,000
Respondents[b]	64,000	106,000	73,000	27,000
Percent	9	13	9	9

[a] These employees are not covered by IRCA's antidiscrimination provision.

[b] These are estimates.

[c] These employers responded that they began or increased asking only foreign-looking or -sounding job applicants to prove they were authorized workers.

[d] These employers responded that they began or increased examining work authorization documents of only foreign-looking or -sounding current workers.

Source: *Ibid*:51.

to warrant a more positive view. While the employer sanctions provisions have been in place for such a short duration and the data still too sketchy to support any firm conclusions about IRCA's effectiveness, a 42 percent reduction in the apprehension of illegal aliens attempting to enter the U.S. is at least suggestive of significant progress. The lack of firm data regarding the degree of discrimination which may have been engendered by the passage and implementation of IRCA is, likewise, still quite problematic. But it would appear that to date, at least, there is little evidence suggesting that the fears of the critics of IRCA are evident; there seems to be no "pattern of widespread discrimination."

This initial assessment of the impact of the employer sanctions provisions of IRCA clearly demonstrate the need for more research and better data upon which to measure the impact. Wage and worker condition data need to be gathered from the DOL to view the impact, if any, of IRCA. Better data on the number of illegal aliens who may still be entering the U.S. is needed, as is a better measure of the increased incidence of the use of fraudulent documents. Some more reliable data on the number of visa overstayers who are still able to circumvent IRCA's employer sanctions provisions need to be gathered and assessed in a rigorous manner. Certainly the evidence from the GAO survey and from comments from relevant nongovernmental agencies suggest there is still a significant underreporting of alleged discrimination practices. Some means to more accurately measure those underreported data would be highly desirable for future research.

FOOTNOTES

1 *See INS Reporter*, January, 1988: 2. For a full discussion of the history of the bill, *See* LeMay, 1989, Chapter 1, or LeMay, 1987, Chapter 6.

2 *See* "Immigration Bill: How a 'Corpse' Came Back to Life," *The New York Times*, Monday, October 13, 1986: A-16; *Congressional Quarterly Weekly Report*, October 18, 1986: 2595-2596; "Conferees Agree on Vast Revisions in Laws on Aliens," *The New York Times*, Wednesday, October 15, 1986: A-1, B-11; and "House Passes Compromise Immigration Bill," *The Washington Post*, Thursday, October 16, 1986: A-5; "Hill Revises Immigration Law," *The Washington Post*, Saturday, October 18, 1986: A-1, 7-8.

3 *See The New York Times*, October 13, 1986: A-16.

4 *CQ Weekly Reports*, October 18, 1986: 2612.

5 *Ibid*, 2596; *See* also *The Washington Post*, Thursday, October 16, 1986: A-5.

6 *See* GAO, 1987, "Report to Congress: Immigration Reform — Status of Implementing Employer Sanctions After One Year," Washington, DC: U.S. Government Printing Office, November. 1987:4, 32.

7 "Abuse of Immigration Law Feared by Some Hispanic Groups," *The New York Times*, March 1, 1987: 31; "Immigration Law Backer Declares Success Amid Other's Doubts," *The Washington Post*, November 6, 1987: A-12; Cohodas, Nadine, "Immigration Law Brings Anxiety, Ambiguity," *Congressional Quarterly*, May 2, 1987: 838-841; "Immigration Rules Called Hard on Poor," *The Washington Post*, April 9, 1987: A-22; "New Law Leaves Immigrants Confused and Fearful," *The New York Times*, February 21, 1987: 29; "New Rules for a Human Tide," *The Economist*, January 17, 1987: 29; "State Panel Faults Enforcement of New Federal Immigration Law," *The New York Times*, March 16, 1987: 15; "Suit Alleges Amnesty Law Puts Many Aliens in Limbo, *The New York Times*, February 17, 1987: 6; "An Illegal Immigrant's Cruel Journey to an Uncertain End," *The Washington Post*, Sunday, November 27, 1988: B1, 10; "Ex-INS Official and Lawyer Indicted," *The Atlanta Journal and Constitution*, Thursday, November 3, 1988: A-1, 19; "Wave of Irish Immigrants Hidden 'Underground'," *The Washington Post*, Sunday, March 12, 1989: A-1, 25; and "Yearn to be Free," *Arizona Republic*, Sunday, January 29, 1989: C-1, 3.

8 "Illegals Fill Day Care Jobs," *The Washington Post*, August 16, 1987: A-1, 16; "Eight Maryland Companies Cited for Illegal Alien Violations," *Cumberland Times/News*, Thursday, September 10, 1987:14; "Maryland Growers Assisting with New Immigration Laws," *The Cumberland Sunday Times*, July 19, 1987: C-12; Weisman, Alan, "Mexican Hearts, California Dreams," *Los Angeles Times Magazine*, September 7, 1987: 7-28; "Farm Work Applications Scrutinized," *Cumberland Times-News*, Tuesday, September 27, 1988: 3; "Illegal Farm Workers Apply for Residency," *Cumberland Times-News*, Thursday, December 1, 1988: 3; "Immigration Stops More Illegal Aliens," *Cumberland*

Times-News, Thursday, March 2, 1989: 1; "INS Breaking Up Smuggling Rings at Airports," *The Washington Post*, Sunday, March 12, 1989: A-24; "Wendy's Pleads Guilty to Hiring Illegal Aliens," *U.S.A. Today*, November 3, 1988: 1.

[9] "Border Attacks Worry INS Agents," *The Washington Post*, Oct. 16, 1988, p. A 18.

[10] "U.S. Immigration Bill Assailed," *The New York Times*, Sunday, October 19, 1986: A-12; "Illegal Migration's Facts of Life, Study Concludes," *The Washington Post*, November 15, 1987: 18; Massey, Douglas, "Understanding Mexican Migration to the United States," *American Journal of Sociology*, 92, May, 1987: 1372-1403; Weisman, Alan, "Mexican Hearts, California Dreams," *Los Angeles Times Magazine*, September 7, 1987: 7-28; "Immigration Law Alone Can't Work," *The Chicago Sun-Times*, April 10, 1987: 1.

[11] INS Reporter, January, 1988: 3; "Wendy's Pleads Guilty to Hiring Illegal Aliens," *U.S.A. Today*, November 3, 1988: 1.

[12] *See*, for example: "Amnesty Program Means Phony Document Business Will Flourish," *The Cumberland Sunday Times*, Sunday, November 2, 1986: A-16; "Reaction to Immigration Bill Is Sharply Split," *The New York Times*, Thursday, October 16, 1986: B-15; "Surge in Bogus Papers Predicted in Wake of Change in Alien Law," *The New York Times*, Monday, October 20, 1986: A-1, 24; and "Immigration Reform: A Mess on the Border," *Newsweek*, December 22, 1986: 27.

REFERENCES

"Abuse of Immigration Law Feared by Some Hispanic Groups," *The New York Times*, March 1, 1987:31.

"A Flood to a Trickle," *The Economist*, March 21, 1987: 22-27.

"Aliens Facing $185 Fee on Amnesty," *The New York Times*, March 16, 1987:15.

"Alien Smuggling Ring Cracked in San Diego," *The Washington Post*, September 28, 1987:A-18.

"Amnesty Program Means Phony Document Business Will Flourish," *The Cumberland Sunday Times*, November 2, 1986:A-16.

"Amnesty Sending Fearful Aliens for Help, Only Some of it Useful,"*The New York Times*, January 15, 1987:B-1,7.

"An Illegal Immigrant's Cruel Journey to an Uncertain End," *The Washington Post*, Sunday, November 27, 1989: B-1, 10.

"A Push to Delay Deportation of Aliens," *The Washington Post*, July 26, 1987:4.

"A Refugee' s Despair,"*Newsweek*, November 17, 1986:12.

Arocha, Zita
1987   "Illegals Fill Day Care Jobs,"*The Washington Post*, August 16:A-1, 16.

Arocha, Zita
1987   "Immigration Law Backer Declares Success Amid Other's Doubts," *The Washington Post*, November 6:A-12.

Arocha, Zita
1988   "INS Reaches Out to Grab Attention on Amnesty," *The Washington Post*, March 27:B-3.

Bernsen, Sam
1987   "Updating the Immigration Law," In *In Defense of the Alien*. Edited by Lydio Tomasi. Staten Island, New York: Center for Migration Studies.

"Border Attacks Worry INS Agents," *The Washington Post*, October 16, 1988:A-18.

"Border Patrol Goes on Alert," *The Washington Post*, July 26, 1987:21.

"Border Attacks Worry INS Agents," *The Washington Post*, October 16, 1988:A-18.

"Canada Moves to Stem Increasing Flow of Aliens Seeking Refuge,"*The New York Times*, February 21, 1987:30.

Church World Service
1987   Immigration and Refugee Program, *Fulfilling the Promise: Church Orientation Guide to the New Immigration Law*. New York: Church World Service, May.

Cohodas, Nadine
1987   "Immigration Law Brings Anxiety, Ambiguity," *Congressional Quarterly*, May 2: 838-841.

"Conferees Agree on Vast Revisions in Laws on Aliens," *The New York Times*, October 15, 1986:A-1, B-11.

Congressional Quarterly Weekly Report, October 18, 1986:2595-2598, 2612-2613.

Congressional Research Service
1986   "Immigration Issues and Legislation in the 99th Congress," Update 12/16/86. Washington, DC: The Library of Congress.

1982   "U.S. Immigration and Refugee Policy: A Guide to Sources of Information," Research Guide JV6201. February 26. Washington, DC: The Library of Congress.

"Eight Maryland Companies Cited for Illegal Alien Violations," *Cumberland Times/News*, November 30, 1987:3.

"Electing to Vote," *The Atlanta Journal and Constitution*, November 3, 1980:A-1, 15.

"Ex-INS Official and Lawyer Indicted," *The Atlanta Journal and Constitution*, November 3, 1988: A-1, 19.

"Farm Work Applications Scrutinized," *Cumberland Times-News*, September 27, 1988:3.

Fragomen, Austin T. Jr.
1975   "Permanent Resident Status Redefined," *International Migration Review*, (9)(1):63-68. Spring.

Fritz, Sara
1988   "New Activists Dilute Power in Congress," *Los Angeles Times*, January 25:1.

General Accounting Office
1987   "Immigration Reform: Status of Implementing Employer Sanctions After One Year," GAO/GGD-88-14. Washington, DC: U.S. Government Printing Office.

1988   "Immigration Reform: Status of Implementing Employer Sanctions After Second Year," GAO/GGD-89-16 Washington, DC: U.S. Government Printing Office.

1982   "Information on the Enforcement of Laws Regarding Employment of Aliens in Selected Countries." Washington, DC: U.S. Government Printing

1987   "Survey of Employer Views of the 1986 Immigration Reform and Control Act," GGD/WBH/11-87 Washington, DC: U.S. Government Printing Office.

"Hill Revises Immigration Law," *The Washington Post*, October 18, 1986:A-1, 7-8.

Hoefer, Michael
1988   "An Interim Report on Aliens Legalizing Under IRCA," Paper Presented at the Population Association of America Annual Meeting, April 23, New Orleans, LA.

"House Approves Compromise Bill on Illegal Aliens," *The New York Times*, October 16, 1986:B-15.

"House Passes Compromise Immigration Bill," *The Washington Post*, October 16, 1986:A-5.

"Illegal Farm Workers Apply for Residency," *Cumberland Times-News*, December 1, 1988:3.

"Illegal Migration's Fact of Life, Study Concludes," *The Washington Post*, November 15, 1987:18.

Immigration and Naturalization Service
1988a Statistical Analysis Branch, Office of Plans and Analysis, "Provisional Legalization Applications Statistics," July.

1988b "Immigration Statistics: Fiscal Year 1987, Advance Report," Washington, DC: U.S. Government Printing Office, June.

"Immigrants: The Changing Face of America," *Time*. Special Edition Issue, July 8, 1985.

"Immigration Commissioner Would Disband Policy Unit," *The Cumberland Times-News*, December 21, 1988:2.

"Immigration: Has Our Melting Pot Boiled Over?" *The Washington Post*, October 18, 1987:D-1, 4.

"Immigration Law Alone Can't Work," *The Chicago Sun-Times*, April 10, 1987:42.

"Immigration Rules Called Hard on Poor," *The Washington Post*, April 9, 1987:A-22.

"Immigration Stops More Illegal Aliens," *Cumberland Times-News*, March 2, 1989:1.

"Immigration Bill Approved; Bars Hiring Illegal Aliens, But Gives Millions Amnesty," *The New York Times*, October 18, 1986:A-1, 8.

"Immigration Bill: How a 'Corpse' Came Back to Life," *The New York Times*, October 13, 1986:A-16.

"Immigration Issues Heats Up Again," *The Washington Post*, Sunday, July 28, 1985:A-15.

"Immigration Legislation Voted Down," *The Cumberland Times/News*, September 14, 1985:A-1.

"Immigration Measure Produces Sharp Division in House Hispanic Caucus," *The Washington Post*, March 18, 1984; A-2.

"Immigration Reform: A Mess on the Border," *Newsweek*, December 22, 1986:27.

"INS Breaking Up Smuggling Rings at Airports," *The Washington Post*, March 12, 1989:A-24.

"INS Ready to Crack Down on Firms That Hire Illegal Aliens," *The Milwaukee Journal*, May 31, 1988:3-A.

"INS Tries New Approach," *The Washington Post*, August 23, 1987:A-1, 18-19.

LeMay, Michael
1987 *From Open-Door to Dutch Door: An Analysis of U.S. Immigration Policy Since 1820*. New York: Praeger

1986 "U.S. Immigration Policy: Entering a Revolving-Door Era?" A Paper Presented at the Annual Meeting of the Midwest Political Science Association, April 8-11, Chicago, Ill.

1985 *The Struggle for Influence*. Lanham, Md.: University Press of America.

Maraniss, David
1988 "Illegal Alien Influx: Illusion vs. Reality," *The Washington Post*, April 24:A-4.

"Maryland Growers Assisting With New Immigration Laws," *The Cumberland Sunday Times*, July 19, 1987:C-12.

Massey, Douglas S.
1987 "Understanding Mexican Migration to the United States," *American Journal of Sociology*, (92):1372-1403. May.

McCarthy, Kevin, and R. Burciaga Valdez
1986   *Current and Future Effects of Mexican Immigration in California;* R-3365-CR. Santa Monica, Cal.: The Rand Corporation, May.

Meissner and Papademetriou
1988   *The Legalization Countdown: A Third Quarter Assessment,* Washington, DC: Carnegie Endowment for International Peace.

"Mexicans Reacting Angrily to U.S. Border Patrol Ditch Plans," *The Cumberland Times-News,* January 28, 1989:3.

"New Law Leaves Immigrants Confused and Fearful," *The New York Times,* February 21, 1987:29.

"New Rules for a Human Tide" *The Economist,* January 17, 1987:29.

Panel on Immigration Statistics
1985   *Immigration Statistics: A Story of Neglect,* Washington, D.C.: National Academy Press.

Passel, Jeffrey S. and Karen A. Woodrow
1984   "Geographic Distribution of Undocumented Immigrants: Estimates of Undocumented Aliens Counted in the 1980 Census by State," *International Migration Review,*(18)(3):642-671.(Fall).

Peters, Ronald M., Jr. and Arturo Vega
1986   "The Role of House Democratic Party Leaders on Non-Party Position Legislation with Partisan Consequences: The Immigration Bill," Paper Presented at the 1986 Meetings of the American Political Science Association, August 28-31, Washington, DC.

"Reaction to Immigration Bill is Sharply Split," *The New York Times,* October 16, 1986:B-15.

"Reagan Said to Favor Signing New Aliens Bill," *The New York Times,* October 17, 1986:A-2.

Refugee Policy Group
1988   "Serving the Newly Legalized: Their Character and Current Needs," Washington, DC.: Center for Policy Analysis and Research on Refugee Issues.

"Salvation by Immigration," *Cumberland Times-News,* October 20, 1988:8

Select Commission on Immigration and Refugee Policy
1981   *Final Report.* Washington, DC.: U.S. Government Printing Office.

Siegel, Passel, and Robinson
1981   "Preliminary Review of Existing Studies of the Number of Illegal Residents in the U.S.," U.S. Immigration Policy and the National Interest: The Staff Report of the Select Commission on Immigration and Refugee Policy, Appendix E: Papers on Illegal Immigration to the U.S. Washington, DC. U.S. Government Printing Office.

"Simpson Tackles Immigration Reform Again," *Minneapolis Star and Tribune,* June 24, 1985:A-10.

"Simpson: the 'Anglo' Behind the Immigration Bill," *The Washington Post,* October 19, 1986:A-8,9.

"Spotlight on Immigration Bill's Cost," *The Washington Post,* October 12, 1986:A-4.

"State Panel Faults Enforcement of New Federal Immigration Law," *The New York Times,* March 16, 1987:15.

"Success Outweigh Failures in First Year of Amnesty Program," *The Washington Post,* November 6, 1987:A-12.

"Suit Alleges Amnesty Law Puts Many Aliens in Limbo," *The New York Times,* February 7, 1987:6.

"Surge in Bogus Papers Predicted in Wake of Change in Alien Law," *The New York Times,* October 20, 1986:A-1, 24.

"The Amnesty Program," *The Washington Post,* May 1, 1988:C-6. "Tragedy Spotlights Immigration Rise," *The Milwaukee Journal,* July 12, 1987:1.

"Trying to Reform the Border," *Newsweek,* October 27, 1986:32,35.

"2,800 Illegal Aliens Arrested in a Weeklong Border Sweep," *The New York Times*, October 20, 1986:A-20.

United States Congress, House of Representatives
1983   "Immigration Reform and Control Act of 1983," The Mazzoli Bill, HR 1510, 98th Congress, 1st Session, February 17:1-163.

U.S. Department of Health and Human Services
1988   "State Legalization Impact Assistance Grant: Eligible Legalized Alien Fact Sheet," Provisional Data, 1989 Projections Texas Department of Health, Bureau of State Health Data and Policy Analysis, July.

U.S. Department of Justice
1988   Immigration and Naturalization Service, INS Reporter, Washington, DC.:U.S. Government Printing Office, January.

"U.S. Immigration Bill Assailed," *The New York Times*, October 19, 1986:A-12. U.S. President's Select Commission on Immigration and Refugee Policy.

U.S. Immigration Policy and the National Interest: Final 1981 Report. Washington, DC: U.S. Government Printing. March.

StaffReport. Washington, DC: U.S. Government Printing Office. April 30.

"Waiting Anxiously: Amnesty Seekers Hope to Prevent Family Separation," *The Dallas Morning News*, January 4, 1988: A-13, 15.

Warren and Passel
1987   "A Count of the Uncountable: Estimates of Undocumented Aliens Counted in the 1980 United States Census," Paper Presented at the 1983 Meeting of the Population Association of America, Pittsburgh, PA., Revised and published in *Demography* (24),(3) August:375-393.

"Wave of Irish Immigrants Hidden "Underground'," *The Washington Post*, March 12, 1989:A-1, 25.

Weisman, Alan,
1987   "Mexican Hearts, California Dreams," *Los Angeles Times Magazine*, September 7, 1987:7-28.

"Wendy's Pleads Guilty to Hiring Illegal Aliens," *U.S.A. Today*, November 3, 1988:1.

Yances, Matt
1988   "Illegal Immigrants Lower Pay of Legal Workers, GAO Says," *The Washington Post*, March 20:H-20.

"Yearn to be Free," *The Arizona Republic*, January 29, 1989:C-1, 3.

21

Employer Sanctions Deserve No Amnesty

PETER A. SCHEY, *Executive Director*
CARLOS HOLGUIN, *General Counsel*
National Center for Immigrants Rights, Inc.[1]

> "I (Jesus) was a stranger and you took me in," (Matthew 25:43)
>
> "Continue to love each other like brothers and sisters, and remember always to welcome the stranger," (Hebrews 13:2)

This article explores the impact of employer sanctions as implemented by the Immigration and Naturalization Service (INS). The authors argue that the employer sanctions law is not measurably reducing the flow of undocumented immigrants and refugees into the United States. Further, although the employer sanctions law is forcing undocumented migrants to accept more unregulated, exploitative and dangerous jobs, and increasing hunger and homelessness among the undocumented, it is not accomplishing its intended goal of driving undocumented workers out of the United States. These migrants and their families would rather remain in the United States, enduring the additional hardships they face here, than return to countries where they may face danger from civil war and even greater poverty.

In addition, the employer sanctions law is harming United States workers. In fact, the law appears to injure the very workers it was intended to benefit: marginally employed minority workers—because these are the very workers most often unable to produce the type of documentation now required of all employees in the United States.

The authors conclude that the employer sanction law is not working. In fact, it is detrimental to the national interest and should be re-examined by Congress. A re-examination should not just focus on whether employer sanctions are causing discrimination against United States minorities, but should also explore the effect the law is having on undocumented workers and the domestic work force as well.

GENERAL REQUIREMENTS OF EMPLOYER SANCTIONS

The Immigration Reform and Control Act of 1986 (IRCA), P.L. 99-603, posits sweeping revisions and additions to the Immigration and Nationality Act, 8 U.S.C. §§1101 *et seq.* (INA) Title I of the IRCA adds §274A to the INA. 8 U.S.C. 1324a. For the first time, federal law proscribes hiring or continuing to employ aliens not authorized by the INS to work in the United States. Employees and prospective employees must produce "documents establishing both employment authorization and identity." 8 U.S.C. §l324a(b)(l)(B). Employers are required to "attest, under penalty of perjury. . .that [they] have verified that [their employees or potential employees] are not. . .unauthorized alien[s]" by examining workers' documents. 8 U.S.C. §1324a(b)(1)(A).

An employee's engaging in unauthorized employment in the United States is at most an administrative violation of the INA, and under some circumstances may not even result in the alien's deportation. However, civil and criminal penalties are imposed against employers who fail to verify employees' documents or who fail to terminate employees unable or unwilling to produce the required documentation. Employers who violate these employment controls face fines of up to ten thousand dollars 8 U.S.C. §1324a(e)(4). Contumacious violators are subject to criminal penalties and civil injunctions. 8 U.S.C. §1324a(f).

In penalizing employers' failure to verify the work authorization of their employees and the employment of unauthorized aliens, the government compels employers' affirmative participation in an indirect border control program; that is, in driving undocumented immigrants and refugees out of the United States by depriving them of employment and, therefore, the ability to obtain the basic necessities of life. In effect, employers are conscripted as policemen, deputized to serve as an adjunct to the INS in carrying out border control.

THE CONSTITUTION AND SANCTIONS

The Government's prerogative to control the borders is not disputed. Employers should not be forced, however, to affirmatively participate in border control efforts of highly questionable effectiveness which also cause injury to domestic and foreign workers alike.

Congress has in essence asked that the public in general, and employers in particular, engage in an act of faith regarding the effectiveness of employer sanctions. INS suggests that the public and employers need not — indeed may not — inquire into the underlying assumptions and methods of implementation of employer sanctions because government may force the citizenry to do whatever it thinks necessary to achieve control of international borders. In INS's view, unless ostensible border control measures are wholly irrational, they may act entirely without constitutional restraint. Even this minimal rationality, it seems, is to be judged not on the basis of empirical facts, but on speculation regarding the importance and utility of the sanctions law.

The Government has made little effort to justify employer sanctions as conferring some tangible public benefit — for example, protecting jobs for United States citizens — of such great importance that the public's and employer's rights not to become unwilling agents of the INS must yield under any set of facts. Rather, in a pending lawsuit filed by the American Friends Service Committee (AFSC) and seven individuals seeking a religious exemption from compliance with employer sanctions, *AFSC* v. *Thornburgh*, No. CV 88-6921-PAR(Kx) (C.D. California), it has argued that regardless of whether employer sanctions do the country any real good, the Government may impose them because it has near-absolute authority to control international borders.

The Constitution, however, is far more practical than the Government would have it, for the "Constitution of the United States was made by, and for the protection of, the people of the United States." *League* v. *De Youna*, 52 U.S. (11 How.) 185, 202, 13 L.Ed. 657 (1850). Accordingly, the Government must justify its actions with more than hollow proclamations of plenary authority: it must show that this authority and the way in which it is exercised yield a tangible benefit adequate to justify curtailing the rights of employers.

The IRCA employment controls go well beyond the Government's controling of borders. When government would coerce the participation of all employers as police investigators, the Constitution guarantees them a just balance between the right to freely hire workers and the Government's need for employers' participation in border control. Fundamentally, this is a balance in which empirical fact, not speculation, must take due priority.

However much the Government would tilt at political or social windmills, it has produced nothing to establish the need for or effectiveness of employer sanctions. At the same time, opposition to employer sanctions is widespread, whether for economic, moral or social reasons. Many employers simply find it repugnant to participate in a system which seeks to drive immigrants and refugees from the United States by causing them to experience hunger and homelessness. Others object to the redtape involved in having to comply with the documentary requirements of employer sanctions. Small businesses, especially minority owned businesses, are displeased because they have taken the brunt of INS's employer sanctions enforcement program. Some employers object to compliance on religious grounds.

Regardless of these objections, as the Government has argued in response to the AFSC lawsuit, in its view "IRCA explicitly makes its proscriptions applicable, *without exception*, to any 'persons or other entity' seeking to hire or continue to employ an individual." Defendants' Motion to Dismiss at 27 n. 7 (emphasis supplied). There is no middle ground on which an employer can contest participation in the employer sanctions program. They must either ignore their objections and comply, or face serious civil and criminal penalties for noncompliance.

We return to the principle that all governmental power flows from the Constitution, and the exercise of such power is therefore subject to constitutional limitations. *Reid* v. *Covert, supra*, 354 U.S. 1, 5-6; 77 S.Ct. 1222 (1957). However much authority the Constitution may grant the Government to itself regulate the admission of immigrants and refugees, it is a different matter where, as is the case here, government turns within to demand the citizenry's affirmative aid in indirect border control efforts. Under such circumstances, the Constitution requires that the Government have at least a rational basis to force such conduct.

Several court decisions establish a distinction historically drawn between the level of constitutional scrutiny applied to governmental actions directed outside, as opposed to inside, the United States.

The Bill of Rights is a futile authority for the alien seeking admission for the first time to these shores, but once an alien lawfully enters and resides in this country he becomes entrusted with the rights guaranteed to all people within U.S. borders. Such rights include those protected by the First and Fifth Amendments and by the due process clause of the Fourteenth Amendment. *See, e.g. Kwong Hai Chew* v. *Colding*, 344 U.S. 590, 596 n. 5; 73 S.Ct. 472 (1953); *accord Landon* v. *Plasencia*, 459 U.S. 21; 103 S.Ct. 321 (1982) ("the power to admit or exclude aliens is a sovereign prerogative. . .however, once an alien gains admission to our country. . .his constitutional status changes accordingly"); *see* also *Scythes* v. *Webb*, 307 F.2d 905, 907-08 (7th Cir. 1962) (First Amendment limitations apply to government's authority to deport an alien for advocating violent overthrow of the government). Clearly, the Government does not wield the same power when addressing issues regarding noncitizens inside the country as contrasted to issues relevant to noncitizens outside the country. Constitutional limits on the Executive's power must be closely guarded in the latter situation. The concept that the Bill of Rights and other constitutional protections against arbitrary government are inoperative when they become inconvenient or when expediency dictates otherwise is a very dangerous doctrine and if allowed to flourish would destroy the benefit of a written Constitution and undermine the basis of U.S. Government. *Reid* v. *Covert, supra,* 354 U.S. 1, 14; 77 S.Ct. 1222 (1957).

The Government's hubristic claim to "near-absolute" power over any matters touching upon immigration should indeed give us pause. No constitutional right could remain inviolate were freedom so readily sacrificed on the putative altar of border control. If the Government's need be great, freedom of choice may yield. But let not Government establish by proclamation what it cannot prove in fact.

DISCRIMINATION AND EMPLOYER SANCTIONS

Congress' determination that employer sanctions be subordinate to its interest in eradicating employment discrimination is apparent throughout IRCA. First, Congress created additional penalties for unlawful employment discrimination so as to preempt the danger of increased discrimination employer sanctions may cause. 8 U.S.C. §1324b.

Generally paralleling Title VII of the Civil Rights Act of 1964, 42 U.S.C. §2000e-2, IRCA's provisions broaden the definition of proscribed discrimination and bar discrimination by smaller employers otherwise exempt from Title VII.[2] This antidiscrimination measure won overwhelming support, passing the House by a margin of 404 to 9. H.R. Rep. No. 682, pt. 1, 99th Cong., 2d Sess., at 69, *reprinted in* 1986 U.S. Code Cong. & Admin. News 5694, 5673.

These efforts reflect Congress' deep concern that employers might use IRCA employment restrictions as a pretext to discriminate on the basis of race. *See* Anti-discrimination Provision of H.R. 3080: Joint Hearing Before the Subcomm. on Immigration, Refugees & Internat'l Law of the House Judiciary Comm. & Subcomm. on Immigration & Refugee Policy of the Senate Judiciary Comm., 99th Cong., 1st Sess. 111 (1985) (statement of Rep. Garcia). Congress emphasized that "every effort must be taken to minimize the potentiality of discrimination and that a mechanism to remedy any discrimination that does occur must be a part of this legislation." H.R. Rep. No. 682, *supra,* at 68, *reprinted in* 1986 U.S. Code Cong. & Admin. News at 5672.

Congress went further still: it required the General Accounting Office to monitor the employer sanctions program and submit three annual reports on whether "a pattern of discrimination has resulted against citizens or nationals of the United States or against eligible workers seeking employment." U.S.C. §1324a(j)(1)(A).[3] This provision reflects Congress' determination that the paramount antidiscrimination interest could be preserved only by "continuous oversight." Hearings on S.529 Before the Subcomm. on Immigration & Refugee Policy of the Senate Judiciary Comm., 98th Cong., 1st Sess. 337 (1983) (statement of Senator Simpson).

Finally, Congress ostensibly retained authority to swiftly end employer sanctions if they resulted in widespread employment discrimination. 8 U.S.C. §1324a(1)(1). This provision is purportedly "a guarantee, built into the statute, that Congress can act expeditiously to rectify any unintended discrimination. If, contrary to all the protections and intentions contained in the bill, new job discrimination does develop...then Congress can sunset employer sanctions." 131 Cong. Rec. S11422 (daily ed. Sept. 13, 1985) (remarks of Senator Kennedy).

Congress, therefore, has made its ordering of priorities unequivocal: however important its interest in employer sanctions, this interest is subordinate to that favoring equal employment opportunity.

Despite this avowed commitment to nondiscrimination expressed by Congress, we believe the federal resources made available by Congress to monitor and remedy such discrimination are completely and utterly inadequate.[4] Add to this the difficulties in proving discrimination, the reluctance of minorities and lawful immigrants to file complaints, and the need for immigrants to file a declaration of intent to become U.S. citizens before coming under the antidiscrimination protections, and it becomes clear that discrimination based on the employer sanctions law, just like discrimination based upon racial hostility or sexism, will go largely undetected and unremedied.

RIGHTS OF THE UNDOCUMENTED UNDER SANCTIONS

In *Sure-Tan, Inc.* v. *N.L.R.B.*, 467 U.S. 883; 104 S.Ct. 2803 (1984), undocumented workers complained their employer had reported them to the INS in order to deter them from engaging in concerted activity protected under 29 U.S.C. §158(a); the workers sought reinstatement and back-pay, the "conventional" remedies for unfair labor practices under §158(a). 467 U.S. at 889. The NLRA provides that an aggrieved worker — without regard to immigration status — may be awarded reinstatement and back-pay as remedies for unfair labor practices. 29 U.S.C. §160(c). Congress, therefore, had not expressly excluded unauthorized workers from receiving these remedies.

The Supreme Court, however, asserted that too literal a reading of the NLRA would bring it into conflict with public policy embodied in the INA, "to preserve jobs for American workers." 467 U.S. at 893. Thus, the Court held, the NLRA should be harmonized with the INA: although undocumented workers are "employees" protected under the NLRA, they may not be ordered reinstated or receive back-pay until they are lawfully admitted to the United States. In short, undocumented workers have a right without an effective remedy. The Supreme Court has left undocumented workers vulnerable to exploitation while virtually inviting unscrupulous employers to take advantage of them with impunity.

This situation is worsened with the enactment of employer sanctions. By all accounts from academicians and service organizations, undocumented workers are not departing the country, nor is the rate of their entry decreasing when those taken out of the migratory cycle through the amnesty program are taken into account.[5] Recent illegal entrants who have been interviewed knew nothing about the employer sanctions law before entering the United States. It therefore played no role in discouraging their entries. However, when questioned about their present difficulties in sustaining themselves, almost all state they would rather work two or three days a week in marginal, unregulated employment in the United States, than experience total unemployment, complete poverty and/or the dangers of civil strife in their home countries. In short, the historical migratory "push" and "pull" factors completely overshadow the difficulties imposed by employer sanctions.

As the impact of employers sanctions takes hold, undocumented workers are increasingly turning to marginalized employment such as day-labor and home piece-work. We have received reports of "women turning to prostitution, "dollar-a-dance" jobs in beer halls, and day-labor house-cleaning jobs in order to feed their children. As locating employment becomes more difficult for undocumented men, they are more frequently than ever before being joined by their undocumented wives who can work illegally, with little chance of detection, as domestics in white middle- and upper-class homes.

Undocumented men and women are increasingly moving into completely unregulated employment relationships, driven even deeper underground by the employer sanctions law. Their access to protective labor legislation, such as federal and state Occupational Health and Safety Acts, minimum wage and over-time laws, is even more attenuated than before. Immigrant and refugee women are increasingly exposed to sexual abuse on the job without being able to turn to any Government agency for protection.

The majority of undocumented workers we have counseled, following enactment of employer sanctions, are aware of the existence of a law criminalizing their employment relationships, but erroneously believe that they, rather than their employers, may be directly penalized under the law. Unscrupulous employers take advantage of this misperception daily, threatening undocumented workers with criminal sanctions if they fail to meet production quotas, or indicate a willingness to complain to authorities about health and safety, or minimum wage violations.

In short, the employer sanctions law is contributing towards the development of a subclass of undocumented, indentured workers in the United States. It is creating with one hand what the amnesty program attempted to cure with the other. The Supreme Court's decision in *Sure-Tan, Inc. v. N.L.R.B.* indicates that the federal courts will provide little protection to the undocumented workers.

IMPACT OF SANCTIONS ON DOMESTIC WORKERS

Employer sanctions injure not only undocumented workers, but also minority, less-educated and marginally employed U.S. workers who are unable to produce the documentation required by INS regulations to obtain lawful employment. Ironically, these are the very workers who supporters of employer sanctions argued would benefit under the new law.

INS regulations provide a list of documents which employees must produce in order to establish their identity and right to be employed in the United States. 8 C.F.R. §274a.2. Most workers, whether here legally or illegally, have never heard of the majority of documents listed in INS's regulations (*e.g.*, Certificate of United States Citizenship, INS Form I-94, Temporary Resident Card, Native American tribal documents, Refugee Travel document).

Unless a worker has a social security card in possession, it is highly unlikely the worker will possess any of the other nine listed documents required to prove entitlement to be employed in the United States. 8 C.F.R. §274a.2(b)(v)(C). Even if a U.S. worker is in possession of a valid social security card, identity must still be proven by presenting a drivers' license, voter registration card or similar document. Of course, many currently unemployed U.S. workers, particularly those who have migrated from rural areas and those with little education, do not possess drivers' licenses, voter registration cards, certified copies of birth certificates or similar documents formally establishing their identity.

Additional burdens are placed on unemployed U.S. workers as a result of the unreasonably short period of time INS regulations allow for acquiring and presenting the required documentation to be lawfully employed. If the potential employee cannot produce the required documentation at the time hired, a receipt showing application for the necessary documents must be produced "within three (3) business days of the hire." Thereafter, the actual documents must be submitted to the employer "within 21 business days of the hire." 8 C.F.R. §274a.2(b)(vi). Many of these documents must be obtained from government agencies often located far from the worker's present residence. It is absurd to require the production of such documents within 21 days when most agencies give a low priority to responding to requests for certified copies of such public records and often take months or even years to respond to such requests. Delays are also frequently encountered because documents have been lost, placed in storage archives or on microfilm, or the requesting party has insufficient information to allow the agency to expeditiously retrieve the requested documents.

Even supporters of employer sanctions have never claimed that undocumented workers are displacing skilled domestic workers or professionals.

The hypothesis, largely unproven, has instead been that undocumented workers, to some immeasurable extent, displace unskilled workers; *i.e.,* minority youth, the unemployed and the marginally employed. However, it is our experience that these are the very workers often unable to readily produce the original documents or certified copies required by INS's regulations. The unemployed must now deal with even more redtape and government agencies just to obtain the documents necessary to end unemployment. Thus, in its implementation, employer sanctions often further discourage the very workers they were supposed to protect.

IMPACT ON UNDOCUMENTED WORKERS

The primary purposes of the employer sanctions law were undoubtedly to reduce the flow of undocumented workers into the United States and at the same time, through denial of access to employment, to force undocumented workers present in the United States to leave the country. It can now be stated with little doubt that the law is not accomplishing either goal.

Organizations which work directly with immigrants and refugees report no reduction in the number of undocumented migrants entering the United States. The National Center for Immigrants' Rights, Inc. (NCIR, Inc.) provides technical assistance and support to approximately six hundred member organizations nationwide. These groups include non-profit organizations, social service agencies, church organizations, and labor unions that provide direct services to immigrants and refugees. These organizational members of NCIR report no measurable reduction in the numbers of undocumented immigrants and refugees seeking assistance since implementation of the employer sanctions law commenced approximately two years ago. The number of clients seeking assistance from NCIR's member organizations has remained relatively constant both before and after the implementation of employer sanctions.

CONCLUSION

No one doubts the Government's power to regulate the circumstances in which persons may enter the United States. The question, however, is whether employer sanctions are likely to achieve the goals they are purportedly designed to serve. The Government's interest in controlling the borders is compelling. But sacrificing equality and dignity in the workplace to an indirect program of marginal efficacy, is a poor constitutional and public policy bargain if domestic workers realize no benefit to outweigh the program's social and moral costs.

Congress would do far more to protect the jobs and working conditions of domestic workers if it granted full labor protections to all workers regardless of immigration status. Such legislation would more than anything else remove the incentive to recruit and hire undocumented foreign labor as all workers would have equal rights before administrative and judicial tribunals adjudicating labor disputes. Congress' refusal or unwillingness to act upon this simple proposition perhaps reflects its relationship with and indebtedness to business and agricultural interests which have historically relied upon cheap foreign labor. This reliance will continue as long as Congress allows employers to extract greater profits by hiring undocumented workers, who can be exploited virtually at will because their employment relationships have been driven deep underground where few regulations matter.

FOOTNOTES

[1] The authors are lead counsel in federal court litigation seeking a religious exemption from compliance with employer sanctions on behalf of a national religious organization and several individual employees and employers.

[2] Congress also created a "special counsel" to prosecute new cases of employment discrimination. 8 U.S.C. §1324b(c). If the special counsel declines to prosecute, Congress determined, an aggrieved employee may pursue a private action. 8 U.S.C. §1324b(d)(2).

[3] The third report must state whether "a widespread pattern of discrimination has resulted . . .solely from the implementation of [employer sanctions]." 8 U.S.C. §1324a(1)(1)(A).

[4] On June 1, 1989, some two years after the employer sanctions law went into effect, the Department of Justice proudly announced that it had just reached "the first settlements (in two cases) of charges alleging that U.S. citizens were discriminated against due to their citizenship status in violation of the antidiscrimination provision of the Immigration Reform and Control Act of 1986 (IRCA)." This dismal record speaks entirely for itself.

[5] See, e.g., "Thousands From the Dominican Republic Brave Stormy Seas for Chance at Better Life," Los Angeles Times, (1989:17. Jan.) Apprehensions of undocumented Dominican boat-people have quadrupled between 1985 and 1989. This "new wave of boat-people" is willing to risk life and limb to come to the United States and escape 25% unemployment and 60% inflation in the Dominican Republic. They give no heed to employer sanctions as they cross the 95-mile turbulent channel to the United States in small, overloaded boats.

22

The Disadvantages of the Sanctions Provisions

ANTONIA HERNANDEZ

President and General Counsel, Mexican American Legal Defense and Educational Fund

The owner of a small company in Southern California, attending a workshop about employers' responsibilities under IRCA, stated that the publicity about the workshop printed in the local chamber of commerce newsletter was the first time she had heard about the I-9 form and its requirements.

January 1989

The owner of this small company is not unlike many others in Southern California and throughout the United States who today remain perilously uninformed of their rights and responsibilities under the Immigration Reform and Control Act of 1986 (IRCA). It is both disheartening and inexcusable that this lack of knowledge is allowed to continue more than two years after the bill was signed into law. Those who have tried to alleviate the problems that exist recognize the immensity of the task. The Mexican American Legal Defense and Educational Fund (MALDEF) continues to oppose employer sanctions because they are unreasonable, unjust and impractical in today's business climate. The disadvantages of the sanctions provisions to both the employer and employee are a high price to pay for negligible returns.

Employers have seen a dramatic change in the role they play because of IRCA — for the first time in history, it is against the law to hire persons not authorized to work in this country. It is against the law; think for a moment what that means. An employer can break the law, be fined and go to jail for "flagrant" violations of one of the most complicated and misunderstood laws of this century. Furthermore, employers have been subjected to this legislative maze even though they do not understand the law and have not been able to get their questions answered. Every time employers call for help, the government phone lines are busy. Employers, in effect, have unwillingly become the front-line of immigration enforcement. If employers have not maintained the proper verification forms on file, if they hire individuals who appear "foreign-looking" or "foreign-sounding," MALDEF research shows that the chances increase ten-fold that these employers will be the target of an I-9 inspection or a workplace raid by the Immigration and Naturalization Service (INS). Of course, if an employer continues to hire undocumented workers the chances of paying the consequences are even more pronounced. Consequently, some employers are having nightmares thinking about the impact of IRCA.

While an employer must act cautiously, the risks for the employee are even greater. Even though a two-phase legalization program was established to provide legal immigration status to undocumented individuals who had either resided in this country since 1982 or had worked as agricultural workers, the program was flawed. MALDEF has gone on record many times criticizing the government for its ineffective and poorly organized outreach efforts on the legalization program. Still it is clear that the employees are the real victims of this law — those who have been fired from their jobs because they previously used a false social security number, cannot get a job because of their appearance, are discriminated against because of their accent, or are deported because even though they are citizens, they "look" undocumented. The adverse impact on the future well-being of these employees is irreversible.

In response to fears of discrimination against authorized workers, nondiscrimination provisions were included in IRCA and a new agency, the Office of Special Counsel (OSC), was established to enforce these provisions. The system designed to deal with these myriad issues is not functioning properly. The provisions protecting the rights of the employee and employer are good intentions gone awry. With the minimal amount of effort put into these provisions, however, we should not be surprised at the results. Like the legalization program, the employer sanctions provisions leave much to be desired in their development, implementation, and interpretation. For example, the nondiscrimination requirements of IRCA are inexplicably narrow both in the categories of individuals protected and in the scope of the employment practices deemed illegal. These requirements were designed to complement the existing body of law barring employment discrimination. Yet why are many people who are authorized to work not protected by the nondiscrimination provisions of IRCA? Because they do not fit into one of four categories of "intending citizens": 1) persons who received amnesty under IRCA's Special Agricultural Workers (SAW) program; 2) applicants for permanent residence; 3) applicants for political asylum; and 4) persons who later filed for amnesty, but who were discriminated against before their applications were filed.

Many of the people who are excluded from coverage under the nondiscrimination provisions do in fact intend to become permanent residents and eventually citizens of the United States. Ironically, they often are especially vulnerable to discrimination because their immigration status means that they do not possess the most common and easily accepted forms of work authorization.

IRCA's nondiscrimination provisions protect workers from discrimination only in certain aspects of the employment relationship; that is, they only apply to practices involving hiring, recruitment, referral for a fee and termination. Discriminatory practices involving the terms and conditions of employment are not covered, although workers have discovered that employers are discriminating against them in terms and conditions of employment. In other words, an employer may pay certain workers less or give them more difficult or dangerous work assignments because they are noncitizens, provided the employees are hired fairly and are not terminated because of their status. Obviously, there are some marked inconsistencies with this policy.

Aside from limited nondiscrimination provisions, authorized workers also are burdened by the numerous mistakes and failures of various government agencies. The INS has failed to issue work authorization in a timely manner to individuals with pending immigration claims. In many instances, wage earners have been terminated by employers who are fearful of sanctions or who refuse to allow the workers time to correct the INS's errors. Other problems with the INS include the failure to promptly replace lost or stolen documents, the issuance of documents with clerical errors which thus make the documents appear fraudulent, and the failure to provide accurate information on the documents acceptable as proof of work authorization.

IRCA regulates the conduct of more than 7 million American employers and the estimated 67.5 million persons, both citizens and noncitizens, hired annually by those employers. IRCA has a widespread effect on the American workplace. The high rates of employer ignorance and of illegal discriminatory practices, found in the second General Accounting Office (GAO) report on the law, inevitably impact hundreds of thousands and perhaps millions of American workers.

The facts as presented in the second GAO report to Congress in November 1988 are painfully clear:

— Twenty-two percent of employers were not aware of IRCA.

— An additional 1.4%, and possibly as many as 7.2% of all employers did not clearly understand one or more of IRCA's major provisions.

— Employers with less than 10 employees were least aware of and least understood IRCA's sanction provisions.

— A private study showed that in January 1988, 61% of all small employers in California and Texas still had not seen the INS *Employer Handbook*, and 56% reported knowing "just a few details" about IRCA.

— Fifteen percent of employers who were aware of and reviewed information on IRCA were unclear about the penalties for employers who discriminate.

— About 50% of employers are voluntarily complying with IRCA's employer sanctions provisions.

— Of the 1.9 million employers, at least 50% had not completed all required I-9 forms. Twelve percent had completed some, but not all, required I-9s; and 38% had not completed any I-9s for the employees they had hired.

Of the 3.3 million employers who were aware of the law, about 528,000 or 16 percent, engaged in illegal discriminatory practices directly related to employer sanctions. There are too many examples of abuses to mention here, but some of these typical actions include:

— Asking only "foreign-looking" or "foreign-sounding" job applicants to present work authorization documents.

— Asking only "foreign-looking" or "foreign-sounding" current employees to present work authorization documents.

— Hiring only U.S. citizens.

— Firing grandfathered employees.

— Requiring aliens to produce a green card.

— Firing legalization applicants who used aliases and/or invalid social security numbers.

— Depriving legalization applicants of seniority and attendant benefits.

— Imposing English-only rules.

Each of these abuses has been repeated time and again since the law was enacted. If each of the 528,000 employers listed in the GAO report dealt with only ten job applicants over the last two years, over 5 million potential employees will have been affected. While it is known that employers are not supposed to engage in these kinds of discriminatory practices, it is quite evident that they do not always know this, and what they do not know is hurting their employees and the United States.

If the business community in the United States was as ignorant about management, marketing and profit margins as they are about the employer sanctions provisions of IRCA, heads would hang in embarrassment for what would surely be an inability to compete effectively in the business world.

The GAO's own survey of employers established widespread ignorance of the law and the use of blatantly illegal discriminatory practices by a significant number of employers. Yet the GAO continues to refuse to conclude that a pattern of discrimination has resulted against authorized workers or that an unnecessary regulatory burden has been created for employers. Employers very clearly are concerned about the hardships their businesses face due to employer sanctions. Employers called the MALDEF immigration toll-free hotline, in operation from January through July 1987, to express their concerns and they continue to contact MALDEF through the agency's California Employer Immigration Education Program which has been in operation since July 1988.

An employee with a small business owner in Northern California presented a picture identification card that was issued by the INS. The employer wanted to know if he could hire the employee because, although the card seemed to indicate that the employee had work authorization, the employer thought that the immigration law required that employees show proof of citizenship.

January 1989

The GAO report accurately identified pervasive discrimination by employers against authorized workers in the United States. Partial blame must be placed on the inadequate educational outreach efforts to the employer by the government. Indeed, the *Handbook for Employers* and the I-9 forms were not printed until after the citation period had begun. And in what perhaps shows the slipshod manner in which the program was implemented, the information was mailed to employers' accountants through a mailing list provided by the Internal Revenue Service and not directly to the employers. Many accountants, unfamiliar with the law, discarded the books and the employers never received the handbooks. MALDEF's files show that many employers still have not received copies of the handbook or the forms.

Today, the contact with employers appears to be minimal with INS agents often dropping off the handbooks and telling the employer, "call us if you have any questions." Equally important, the handbook virtually ignores the nondiscrimination provisions of IRCA. In its nearly 20 pages, the book devotes less than one page to IRCA's nondiscrimination provisions. Is it any wonder that there is an information gap among the employers?

Moreover, the GAO report failed to acknowledge all of the burdens that have been imposed on employers by IRCA. For example:

— The annual cost of completing the forms is estimated to be 182 million dollars by the INS and 675 million dollars by the Small Business Administration.

— Company personnel must learn the finer points of IRCA to avoid discrimination and to keep up with changes that develop with regard to this evolving law. For smaller companies, this may require a new salaried employee.

— The costs of defending charges of discrimination and notices of intent to fine by the INS can be expensive.

— The cost of replacing experienced employees, who are grandfathered and eligible to work, but vulnerable to deportation through a raid (and therefore sometimes discharged to avoid this risk) must also be accounted.

The GAO also has not indicated how many cases of discrimination it believes would constitute a "widespread pattern of discrimination" as a result of employer sanctions. If job discrimination has developed, despite the protections and intentions contained in the bill, Congress in all good conscience must sunset employer sanctions. Therefore, a definitive determination must be made on what constitutes widespread discrimination.

In the past, the courts have found and struck down discriminatory policies based on proof of existence of the policies alone without examining the number of victims. For example, in *United States* v. *Bob Lawrence Realty*, the evidence that two real estate agents had made prohibited representations to four individuals was sufficient to sustain a finding of a "pattern or practice" of FHA violations by all agents in the area. In *United States* v. *Gilman*, two instances of housing discrimination by the management of an apartment building were sufficient. At least 286 charges of discrimination have been filed with the OSC, and interested groups have produced substantial anecdotal evidence of additional instances of discrimination. The facts show that a pattern and practice of employment discrimination have developed due to employer sanctions. The GAO must focus on the level of discriminatory activity in industries or regions where large alien populations make such discrimination a possibility, as well as the aggregate level of discrimination at the national level.

There are other problems that exist in the implementation of IRCA: the rules governing petitions for naturalization under IRCA (the six-month requirement unfairly excludes many aliens), the obstacles to the declaration of intending citizen (the old original form was no longer in use and the newer form was unavailable) and interpretations of various statutes and the difficulty in getting necessary forms filed (INS local offices still have no uniform procedure in processing the I-772).

Proposed Corrective Measures

Because there is extreme concern that the issues raised are addressed in a thorough and timely fashion, MALDEF proposes the following corrective measures:

— The establishment of OSC regional offices as authorized by IRCA. This undoubtedly has affected the number of individuals who have made claims of employment discrimination.

— As INS increases sanctions enforcement, it becomes exceedingly important to educate the public about IRCA's antidiscrimination provisions. Additional supplemental appropriations for FY 1989 and FY 1990 for the OSC are essential if persons discriminated against are to know about the legal remedies in IRCA. The effort should target employers, employees, potential employees and victims of discrimination.

— The INS must be disengaged from its dual role as educator of employers and enforcer of the law. The inappropriateness of this arrangement is apparent. An INS agent's observations during an "educational" visit may be used in an affidavit to secure a search warrant to later conduct a disruptive workplace raid. Changes must be made in this bureaucratic irregularity.

— A moratorium of employer sanctions should be imposed through the duration of this public education campaign and there should be a return to the citation and education phase of employer sanctions and antidiscrimination implementation.

— Technical and clarifying corrections to IRCA's antidiscrimination provisions must be made to expand the OSC's jurisdiction to include discrimination concerning wages, hours, promotions or conditions of employment.

— All discriminatory practices based on the use of the I-9 form must be linked to employer sanctions. It is clear that in the absence of the I-9 verification process, the discrimination would not have occurred.

— The intending citizen requirement must be dropped as a prerequisite to IRCA's antidiscrimination protections.

— IRCA's antidiscrimination protections must be extended to applicants for refugee, asylum and permanent resident status, and to SAWs.

— The antiretaliation protection for victims of IRCA discrimination must be codified.

— Discrimination should be broadly defined to include any discriminatory practices that violate Title VII or other federal (or state) laws prohibiting employment discrimination, whether or not a victim has brought a charge.

Perhaps one of the main drawbacks of this immigration legislation is that it gives individuals a false sense of security and control over U.S. borders. Anyone who has seriously studied the causal factors of immigration to the United States knows that this law is not the panacea it was promoted to be by the legislators who sponsored it, by those who signed it and by those enforcing it. The law does not take into account the economic realities of the immigration question and without this consideration, the issue cannot be resolved. The Select Committee on Immigration and Refugee Policy in 1981 recommended immigration control premised on employer sanctions, a proposal which would purportedly destroy the "magnet" that draws "illegal" immigrants to this country by penalizing employers who knowingly hire unauthorized workers. This law has not been effective. While the INS boasts that apprehensions at the border have decreased, this is easily explained by the fact that immigrants are not crossing as frequently as they did in the past because they are staying on this side of the border. The undocumented continue to enter, reside and work in the United States, and anyone who thinks otherwise is not facing the real issues.

Preliminary monitoring by various agencies and community organizations across the nation also suggests that rather than eliminating exploitation, IRCA may be driving the undocumented even further underground and creating a whole new class of immigrants so desperate for work that they will accept increasingly substandard wages and working conditions. A recent *New York Times* article reported that "a half-million illegal aliens form what amounts to a new subclass of the poor, more vulnerable than ever to sweatshop operators, eviction and criminals." Agencies also have reported instances where employers have preferred undocumented employees over work authorized employees, thus undermining the force IRCA may have as a means of regulating those who are not work authorized. Another common scenario is that the newly legalized are being fired and the undocumented are replacing documented workers in the workplace.

A small business in Arizona required all its employees to present work authorization documents and complete I-9 forms. When some workers, who had been hired before November 1986, could not produce such documents, they were fired.

October 1988

As the GAO gears up for its third and final report to Congress, the time has come to realistically assess the effects of the United States' experiment in immigration reform. Very few are willing to look critically at this law, to recognize and admit that immediate firm policy intervention is required. IRCA's purported reform jeopardizes the livelihood of too many minority or "ethnic-looking" United States citizens and newly legalized immigrants. It also has created an unnecessary regulatory burden for employers. After a close analysis of the effects of the implementation of IRCA, it is time to reconsider employer sanctions and end the disturbing wave of IRCA-related employment discrimination.

23

The Impact of IRCA's Employer Sanctions Provision on Workers and Workplace

MUZAFFAR A. CHISHTI

Director
Immigration Project, International Ladies Garment Workers Union

This paper addresses the issue of the impact of the employer sanctions provisions of the Immigration Reform and Control Act of 1986 (IRCA) on workers and on the workplace. More specifically, the implication of the law on labor rights and protections, the behavior of employers and the labor market and recruitment process will be discussed.

In enacting IRCA, Congress — perhaps unintentionally — also affected general developments in labor law. IRCA does not just touch immigrants, it affects every single worker in the United States. In addition, IRCA concerns not only the employers of illegal immigrants, but all employers. Employers who have never interacted with immigrants before are now asked to adhere to the extremely tedious provisions of IRCA. Thus, after IRCA, employer-employee relations in the United States have been altered in a very fundamental way.

For the sake of simplicity, the universe of employers may be divided into three categories: employers who obey laws (or at least want to claim that reputation); employers who habitually violate laws and know full well that the enforcement mechanism is too slow or too overburdened to apprehend them; and employers who, once again, habitually violate laws but are less confident about the inadequacy of the enforcement mechanism. All three categories of employers present a problem in the context of IRCA.

The first category of employers — the good reputation or "legal" employers — frequently operate in the primary sector of the economy. They have options among potential recruits. They could easily hire a fourth-generation American, or a recently-arrived lawful permanent resident from Mexico. Not to take any chances with exposure to sanctions under IRCA, it is likely that such employers will simply play it safe and hire "unquestionably" American-looking or sounding workers. The potential for discrimination is real. Recent studies by the Inter-agency task forces in New York City and Chicago, and the interim study by the General Accounting Office (GAO) raise significant concern about the extent of discrimination that has already taken place.

The second category of employers — the astute, unscrupulous employers — see IRCA as yet another law to break. But in this instance, these employers have an additional advantage. They are astute enough to know that given the structure and funding of the Immigration and Naturalization Service (INS), their chances of being caught at breaking the law are minimal. They can, however, use the possibility of a sanction as a potent weapon against the undocumented worker. The wage of the worker may be reduced by simply arguing that money is needed as an "insurance policy" against fines for hiring the worker. The worker, already vulnerable, cannot afford to complain. Evidence of this behavior has already come to the attention of unions. Employers, conveniently, have chosen to become the enforcers of the law.

The third category of employers — the classic sweatshop operators — may not be astute enough to know the limitations of INS enforcement policy. These employers may actually be afraid of being caught violating the new law. If this group of employers now operate their sweatshops in back alleys, employer sanctions will eventually drive them completely underground. Thus, law enforcement officers from the Department of Labor, and health and safety inspectors as well, will find it difficult to monitor the conditions in these shops.

Given the exploitative condition of these workers, where do they turn for protection? In the past, undocumented workers could seek the membership and protection of unions. Unfortunately, the new law adversely influences the ability of unions to organize and protect undocumented workers. If undocumented workers sign union cards, they may be fired but have no recourse. Prior to IRCA, this would have been an unfair labor practice. Post-IRCA, the union is defenseless: the employer, after all, cannot be asked to reinstate a worker who cannot lawfully work. Thus, employers will continue to hire the undocumented as long as it is suitable — at a low wage — and discharge them when it becomes inconvenient. Ironically, therefore, employer sanctions may achieve the exact opposite of the intended goal: depress wages and working conditions rather than improve them.

Employer sanctions have had an adverse impact on employee recruitment practices in an industry like garment manufacturing. In the apparel industry, like other segments of the secondary sector economy, immigrant workers constitute a significant part of the workforce and method of recruitment is mostly informal. Available positions do not get advertised in the classified columns, they are filled through informal networks. The word-of-mouth network in the ethnic enclaves generates the needed supply of labor. Prior to IRCA, the informal network supplied workers both to "legal," and to "illegal," or sweatshop operations. Since the employers were not required to check documentation, the undocumented workers that came through the informal networks also found themselves in the "legal" shops, working side by side with documented workers. After IRCA, however, the "legal" employers have to check documents. They, therefore, find themselves rejecting the undocumented workers that come through the informal networks. The undocumented worker, lacking choices, gravitates toward the "illegal" or the sweatshop sector. The "legal" employer, now forced to rely on the formal method for recruitment, finds this mechanism unable to produce the needed workers. Thus, the legal sector is experiencing a shortage of workers, while the illegal sector has had the supply increased.

Before IRCA, both the legal and illegal sectors competed for the same workers. Thus, in an interesting way, the legal sector had some ability to set the wages and work standards for all workers — including undocumented workers. In the absence of competition, the illegal sector is now free to set its own conditions for undocumented workers. Thus, employee recruitment has become more difficult for "legal" shops, and considerably easier for the "illegal" operations.

If employee recruitment has become more difficult for the "legal" employers, as a result of employer sanctions, they face two options: close their businesses in the United States and move them abroad, or make a concerted demand for large-scale importation of temporary foreign workers. Neither of these two options would be desirable, however, as part of the long-term national policy. It is not in the interest of the United States to allow an important part of its manufacturing base to be permanently exported. Nor is it prudent for the United States, to institutionalize a program that relies on a large pool of temporary foreign workers. Experience with such programs in the agriculture sector, and with the guestworker programs in Europe, is enough to provide grounds for pause and reflection on the long-term implications of IRCA.

Thus, the effectiveness of the employer sanctions mechanism should be reviewed in the context of the realities of the labor market, and not on the basis of strong passions that surround the debate on illegal immigration.

APPENDIX

Program of the CMS Twelfth Annual National Legal Conference on Immigration and Refugee Policy

Sponsored by:
The Center for Migration Studies of New York, Inc. at the
Capital Hilton Hotel, Washington, D.C.
April 6-7, 1989

PROGRAM ━━━━━━━━━━━━━━━━━━━━━━━━━━━━━━

THURSDAY, APRIL 6, 1989

7:45 a.m. - 8:45 a.m.	FINAL REGISTRATION WELCOME **Lydio F. Tomasi,** c.s., Executive Director, The Center for Migration Studies

9:00 a.m.	## SESSION I: IMPACTS AND CONSEQUENCES OF THE IMMIGRATION AND CONTROL ACT OF 1986 (IRCA)

Chair:	**Msgr. Nicholas DiMarzio,** Executive Director, USCC Migration and Refugee Services, Washington, D.C.
Panelists:	"Legalization and Related Issues (Systematic Alien Verification for Entitlement, etc.): An Overview" **Frank D. Bean,** Urban Institute, Washington, D.C. "Legalization Implementation: Phase 2" **Raymond Penn,** INS Assistant Commissioner for Legalization "Reported Fraud in the Implementation of IRCA: A Government Response" **John F. Shaw,** INS Assistant Commissioner for Investigations "Technical Amendments to the Immigration Law" **Crystal L. Williams,** Director, AILA's Legalization Appeals Project
Discussion:	

10:30 a.m.-12:30 p.m. SESSION II. LEGALIZATION, SOCIAL
SERVICES AND HEALTH

Chair: **Sonia M. Leon Reig,** Director, Migrant Health Program, H.H.S.

Panelists: "Bringing Immigrants into the Health Care System"
John W. McFarland, Chair, Migrant Clinicians Network

"Impacts of IRCA/SLIAG on Public Education: The California Experience"
Linda J. Wong, Executive Director, California Tomorrow

"Integrating Immigrants into the Labor Market and Labor Unions"
Aaron Bodin, INS Assistant Commissioner
Dick Wilson, AFL-CIO, Washington, D.C.

Discussion: **Louis Caraballo,** IRCA Program Executive
Thomas Joseph, National Association of Counties

12:30 p.m.- 2:00 pm. AWARDS LUNCHEON PROGRAM

Presiding: **The Honorable Diego Asencio,** Chairman, C.S.I.M.C.E.D.

Invocation: **Most Rev. Pio Laghi,** Apostolic Nuncio to the U.S.

Speaker: **Augusto Ramírez-Ocampo,** UN Development Programme

Benediction: **Donald H. Larsen,** Director, Lutheran Immigration and Refugee Services

2:00 p.m. - 3:30 p.m. SESSION III. REVISION OF U.S. LEGAL
IMMIGRATION SYSTEM

Chair: **Charles B. Keely,** Georgetown University

Panelists: "Immigration Reform and the Needs of Business"
Austin Fragomen, Chairman, American Council on International Personnel

"Toward a Selection System"
Doris M. Meissner, Carnegie Endowment for International Peace

"Immigration Reform: A Government Perspective"
Richard E. Norton, INS Associate Commissioner

"A Global Approach to Immigration Reform"

Dale Frederick Swartz, President, The National Immigration, Refugee &
Citizenship Forum

Discussion: **Richard Scott** — GAO
Dan Stein — FAIR

| 3:30 p.m.- 5:30 p.m. | **SECTION IV. THE UNFINISHED BUSINESS OF LEGAL IMMIGRATION REFORM:ISSUES IN NEED OF FURTHER ANALYSIS** |

Chair:	**David Martin,** University of Virginia School of Law
Panelists:	"Reforming the Criteria for the Exclusion and Deportation of Alien Criminal Offenders **Stephen H. Legomsky,** Washington University School of Law
	"Reform of Political Exclusion Policy" **Susan R. Benda,** American Civil Liberties Union
	"Post-82 Undocumented Aliens" **Richard Ryscavage, S.J.** — USCC Migration and Refugee Services
Discussion:	Other Recent Developments and Congressional Proposals on Legal Immigration and Related Topics **Warren Leiden** — AILA

| 6:00 p.m.- 9:00 p.m. | **RECEPTION, Cafe Italiano 1129 Pennsylvania Avenue** |

FRIDAY, APRIL 7, 1989

| 9:00 a.m.-10:45 a.m. | **SESSION V. REFUGEES; INTERNATIONAL PERSPECTIVES** |

Chair:	**Dale S. de Haan,** Director, Immigration & Refugee Program, C.W.S.
Panelists:	"Perestroika and Refugees from USSR" **Judith Golub,** AJC, Washington, D.C.
	"Hong Kong, Cuba and Haiti: From Refugee Emergencies to Migration Flows" **Robert L. Bach,** State University of New York, Binghamton
	"Monitoring Repatriation: Afghan and Central America" **John McCallen,** UNHCR, Washington, D.C.
	"Private Sector Sponsorship" **Wells Klein,** American Council for Nationalities Services
Discussion:	

| 10:30 a.m.-12:30 p.m. | **SESSION VI. REFUGEES:DOMESTIC POLICY ISSUES** |

| Chair: | **Karl Zukerman,** The Hebrew Immigration Aid Society |

Panelists: "'Humanitarian Refugees' and the Need for a Safe Haven Policy"
                      Arthur C. Helton, Director, Political Asylum Project, Lawyers
                      Committee for Human Rights

                      "Asylum Claims from a Judicial Perspective"
                      Judge William R. Robie, Chief Immigration Judge, U.S. Department of Justice

                      "Revisiting the Refugee Act: Prospective Changes"
                      Jerry Tinker, Subcommittee on Immigration and Refugee Affairs, U.S. Senate

Discussion

12:30 p.m.-2:00 p.m. DELI BUFFET LUNCHEON —
                      South American Room

2:00 p.m.-5:00 p.m.   SESSION VII. IRCA'S EMPLOYER SANCTIONS
                      PROVISIONS:

Have they been carried out satisfactorily? Have they caused a pattern of discrimination against workers? Have they caused unnecessary regulatory burdens on
employers? Are they in the public interest?

Chair: **Roy S. Bryce-Laporte,** C.I.P.S., College of Staten Island, C.U.N.Y.

Panelists: **John R. Schroeder,** INS Assistant Commissioner

                      Lawrence Siskind, Special Counsel for Discrimination

                      Arnold P. Jones, U.S. General Accounting Office

                      Bruce Bushart, State Coordinator — New York State Department of Social Services

                      Georges Vernez, The RAND Corporation

                      Michael C. LeMay, Political Science, Frostburg State University

                      Peter A. Schey, Executive Director, National Center for Immigrants' Rights, Inc.,
                      Los Angeles

                      Antonia Hernandez, President, MALDEF

                      Muzaffar Chishti, International Ladies Garment Workers Union

                      Richard Day, Sub-Committee on Immigration and Refugee Policy, U.S. Senate

Discussion and Conclusions:

PROGRAM ORGANIZING COMMITTEE:

Lydio F. Tomasi, Chairman; Graziano Battistella; Austin T. Fragomen, Jr.;
Nicholas DiMarzio; Charles B. Keely; Mark Miller; Silvano Tomasi.

Index